This book is to be
the last dat

Library Services
Victoria Buildings
Queen Street
Falkirk
FK2 7AF

709
.2
MCKI

Falkirk Council

Colin Baxter Photography Limited, Grantown-on-Spey, Scotland

First published in Great Britain in 1998 by
Colin Baxter Photography Ltd, Grantown-on-Spey, Moray, Scotland
Revised 2000
Revised 2001
Text Copyright © John McKean 1998, 2000, 2001
Photographs Copyright © Colin Baxter 1998
All rights reserved

www.colinbaxter.co.uk

Front Cover Photograph: The Room de Luxe, Willow Tea Rooms
Back Cover Photograph: Stencil in Main Bedroom, Windyhill
Page 2 Photograph: Detail, Bedroom Fireplace, The Hill House
Page 72 Photograph: Gentlemen's Cloakroom Door, Glasgow School of Art

ISBN 1-84107-110-2

Printed in Hong Kong

Charles Rennie
MACKINTOSH
Pocket Guide

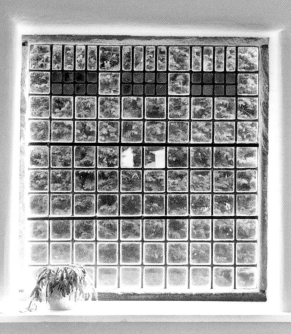

BIOGRAPHY

Charles Rennie Mackintosh (1868 - 1928) today offers a defining image of Glasgow. The work he completed in his native city, around a century ago, is known round the world. A major exhibition of his work toured the USA in 1996-7; his graphic imagery is mercilessly reproduced, his designed objects are copied and regurgitated, and now his interior spaces and even complete buildings are cloned.

The Charles Rennie Mackintosh Society is more than a powerfully active supporters' club. A fine interpretation of Mackintosh is a permanent display at The Lighthouse, which was formed in 1999 within the shell of Mackintosh's *Glasgow Herald* building in Mitchell Street. For the visitor to Mackintosh, the Society's headquarters at Queen's Cross, or The Lighthouse are obvious first ports of call.

Almost all Mackintosh's small architectural œuvre, as well as much of his furniture and decorative or illustrative work, is in and around Glasgow. But his brightly-lit fame these days also forces us all to judge for ourselves: to see what Mackintosh actually designed, through the layers which have been washed away from – or added to – his works.

By the 1920s there was a typical Mackintosh interior next door to his Willow Tea Rooms; it has vanished, and no-one today knows if it was an earlier, genuine Mackintosh or not. While today, in the Blue Room, upstairs in 'The New Willow Tea Rooms' in Buchanan Street (designed 50 years after his death), there is some very tasteful reconstruction, like the low 'Chinese' chairs; alongside which a tall-backed chair appears – but in a display case, as an exhibit. How confusing! Moreover many of Mackintosh's fitments were copied in his lifetime, can be again today, and anyway the originals are easily moved: the cover of one book on the Glasgow School of Art is an illustration of the stair light

◀ *Throwing light in a Mackintosh interior. The purity, simplicity and subtle charm of the little drop pendant over the square porch window at Windyhill (1900), with its 10 by 10 leaded squares.*

from a Mackintosh house which happens now to be in the Art School collection.

But Mackintosh was not the lone martyr whose life deserves memorialising with all the accoutrements, the sale of relics and the tawdry memorabilia of a local saint. He was a tirelessly inventive designer and, more importantly, a great architect. Much of his work was shared with his lifelong and devoted partner Margaret Macdonald, an artist and very talented designer in her own right. They, along with another couple, Margaret's sister Frances and Herbert McNair, were for a very brief time, exactly a century ago, known as 'The Four'. This quartet was deeply embedded in a much wider group of innovative and lively designers and artists of the Glasgow Style. This wider style was closely influenced by nationalist and Celtic revivalist ideas in Scotland, by the Arts & Crafts and the Aesthetic Movements in England, and not least by the great centres of European contemporary design of the moment, most obviously fin-de-siècle Vienna.

Mackintosh aged 25, photographed by Annan in 1893 not as the assistant architect but as the interior artist.

The extraordinary, sudden and brief flowering of art nouveau across Europe and even the USA around 1900, gave Mackintosh a sudden fame as decorator of the artistic interior. Even before the bright flame of that fashion went, as quickly as it came, Mackintosh had outgrown it, to become one of the few great original architects of the time.

In the late 1880s, the young Mackintosh had entered a double world – the practical, masculine and dour world of construction, and the bright, romantic and feminine world of art. An apprentice architect by day, his evenings and weekends were spent with friends wrapped in symbolic and allegorical image making. They called themselves 'The Immortals', and within this group were formed The Four. The few formative years of their intense collaboration in the mid 1890s were of great importance. Mackintosh and Margaret married in 1900 and the work became inextricable; he would sign drawings 'CRM – MMM'. (The use of one set of initials in this text always recalls the unspoken other half of this double signature.)

Macdonald, in an 1899 CRM chair, probably photographed before their marriage in 1900.

In 1893, having assisted and detailed various buildings and extensions in the office of Honeyman & Keppie, CRM designed the first new building we recognise as his: the Glasgow Herald warehouse (now The Lighthouse). This, and the Martyrs' School which followed in 1895 (p57), both show glimpses of unusual talent, but neither is architecturally remarkable. At the same time, he began designing furniture, if not yet with an individuality we recognise as his own.

In 1896, Honeyman & Keppie was invited to compete for Glasgow's new Art School. One of their entries, clearly designed by 28-year-old Mackintosh, won (p18). The governors only had money for half, which was built over three years and opened at the end of 1899. Later, they decided to complete the project, and Mackintosh, now fully in control, completely revised a new west end. Finished exactly a decade later, this masterpiece was virtually both his first and his last building. CRM's architectural work is almost all that of a man in his thirties.

As the School of Art was rising, with John Keppie running the job on site (and even claiming the design as his), CRM continued to produce furniture and illustration on his own. In 1896, the commission to stencil decoration for a tea room in Buchanan Street started CRM's long association with his most faithful patron, Kate Cranston. He designed her no new buildings; simply a wonderful succession of tea room interiors, furniture, decoration, cutlery and even waitresses' costumes, in existing city-centre blocks. He also refitted and furnished her own Glasgow house. Most of all this invention is now lost, and none – apart from the first floor of one tea room – remains in place today.

In 1897, while in the daytime as architect designing his only church (p31), CRM's other life as Artist was first noticed; *The Studio* illustrated a mural and some furniture. Then, alongside the small Ruchill church hall (p33), came much furniture for Miss Cranston's tea room at 114 Argyle Street. His range of seating and light-fittings here includes the famous dark oak chairs, with their tall back legs and two vertical flats ending in an oval disc above the seater's head through which a bird flies (p63).

In the last days of the century, the Art School, an odd half-building, was opened, filled and fitted with CRM's latest furniture and interior ideas including the masterly Director's suite. He now designed the printing office for another local paper, *The Daily Record* which, like the earlier *Glasgow Herald* building, required only a conventional block and got an unconventional skin. At the same time, in the utterly contrasting location

▶ *The rose was the central symbol of the Glasgow Style around 1900, taken to its most abstract and graphic, as well as its widest range of representation, by CRM-MMM. From their Rose Boudoir in Turin in 1902, it is echoed in MMM's gesso panels, in inlaid furniture, metalwork at the School of Art, lightfittings and leaded glass, stencilling on chair upholstery and around interior walls. This example is on a bookcase for Windyhill (1901) now in the Glasgow School of Art.*

of an open suburban hillside, Mackintosh designed his first large detached house. In Kilmacolm, 14 miles (22.5 km) south-west of Glasgow, Windyhill was also his first building whose exterior image seemed entirely based on a harled, unornamented Scottish vernacular. This important house has turned its back successfully to the public since it was built, and it holds its privacy to this day. (It is almost always illustrated by a photograph of the back, and is not accessible to the public.)

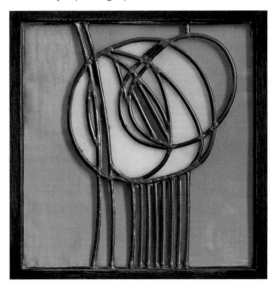

When they married in 1900, MMM and CRM fitted out their own first-floor apartment at Blythswood Square (p61) and then, in Ingram Street, created their first large-scale tea room interior, the Ladies' Luncheon Room. Late that year, The Four were invited by Josef Hoffmann, the Viennese architect, and his colleagues J M Olbrich and Gustav Klimt, to take part in a Vienna Secession exhibition. CRM later called it the trip of his lifetime. The Mackintoshes designed their own room, and filled it with both the atmosphere of their new flat and some real pieces of their home furniture. The exhibition was praised and became influential among designers; CRM furniture was fitted into a Hoffmann-designed house.

While there, the Mackintoshes heard about and entered a German publisher's competition for 'a house for an art lover.' Although their entry could not be considered a winner because it was incomplete, when the sponsor published portfolios of the three best projects, one was the Mackintosh. Thus it was possible that, nearly a century later, this dream house is somewhat realised in Bellahouston Park (p36). Meanwhile, back in the real world, Mackintosh got down to detail design at Windyhill, whose shell was nearly built – forming its interior spaces, fitments and

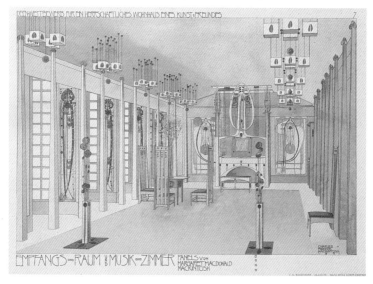

fittings – and he entered the competition for a vast Liverpool Cathedral in which he was not placed.

In 1902, they exhibited again in Europe (in Turin), and a German magazine published the most serious account of the Mackintoshes' work that would appear in their lifetimes. This publication also included the design for an Artist's Cottage in the country – one of a couple of abstract, client-free projects of great simple charm. (These drawings have also recently been used as the basis of a reconstruction, near Inverness.) Francis Newbery, head of the Glasgow School of Art, organised the 'Scottish section' in Turin; CRM was architect and, with MMM, created the exquisite room setting 'The Rose Boudoir'. Invitations to exhibit in Dresden, Moscow and Berlin (if not in Britain) soon followed. In Vienna, the Mackintoshes used their collaborative skills to produce their most complete artistic interior – a music room for Fritz Wärndorfer, a wealthy Secessionist supporter. Now CRM's domestic masterpiece The Hill House was being designed (p39) and the finest tea rooms, The Willow (p52), begun.

In mid-1903, while The Willow was being fitted out, CRM landed the job of a large new Glasgow board school in Scotland Street (p58). Then, while that school was going up, he created the interiors of The Hill House and those for the main rooms of Miss Cranston's old southside mansion, Hous'hill. Here he had a free hand with the interiors, creating half a dozen complete room settings, and even more furniture than for The Hill House. (The interiors for Wärndorfer were dispersed or destroyed by 1916; at Hous'hill it was another 15 years before the furniture was dispersed (mostly lost) and the house and its fitments then demolished by its owners, Glasgow Corporation, after a fire. All we have of either are one or two endlessly reproduced photographs.)

It is difficult in a short tale to avoid the impression that there was no local context within which the Mackintoshes lived and worked. There were obviously artistic and architectural allegiances as well as enmities. A visit to the Art Galleries, being built at the same time as the Art School, gives a good turn-of-the-century context. This building itself is both overwhelming and vulgar. An 1892 competition-winner, by English academic architects Simpson & Allen, it beat 24-year-old CRM's eclectic and highly decorated juvenile extravaganza, as well as Honeyman's mediocre neo-Greek and Keppie's conventional and clumsy Beaux-Arts entries.

Six years later, for the International Exhibition of 1901 to be sited alongside the new Art Galleries,

◄ *Music and reception room in the House for an Art Lover. As CRM's ceilings usually do, this one vanishes; here the avenue of tapering posts just touches the vault with tiny green leaves. Between the bay windows and this line of posts, he drops a rail which hides the window-heads, and binds this long space within its aesthetic grove.*

a more mature and independent CRM competed for the buildings. While the winners were again all elaborately decorated wedding cakes, in keeping with the Art Galleries, CRM had now abandoned all that baggage. His beautiful drawings rely on subtle curves and simple forms. His 'alternative concert hall' proposal, with its coolly shaped shallow dome to seat 4221, shows the contrast best.

▶ *Mackintosh drew flowers all his life, but was particularly prolific during his stay in Walberswick, Suffolk, from 1914 to 1915. It was there that he made this exquisite study of* Fritillaria. *The plant's chequered petals are actually precisely observed, though they might seem (as nature following art) to be created as a CRM stylisation.*

Relics from 1901 are still to be found inside the Art Galleries – room settings by E A Taylor, John Ednie, George Logan and George Walton, fine Glasgow Boys paintings, a beautiful Talwin Morris mirror which had been at the Turin 1902 exhibition, and there are CRM candlesticks and cutlery, alongside as much as they can show of his Ingram Street tea room furniture.

By 1904 however, art nouveau was as past as the mysterious, grotesquely attenuated figures in the 'spook school' paintings of The Four. The changing architectural context is shown in the work of James Salmon, which develops astonishingly from 'The Hatrack' (1899-1902), Glasgow's finest art nouveau block in Bath Street, to Lion Chambers (1904-7), a stern reinforced-concrete block in Hope Street. Salmon and his good friend Mackintosh (or 'wee Troutie' and 'Toshie' as they were known) used to be annoyed (I quote Salmon) 'that nobody else is proud enough of Glasgow to be ashamed of it.' Salmon's relationship with a more classical and less inventive partner, remarkably similar to CRM's experience, was to end in 1913.

In the first decade of the century, CRM was at the peak of his career. He moved up in the world with MMM from their rented flat to purchase a terrace house in the West End, in a fashionable middle-class suburb by the university. This building, offering the closest contact with their domestic intimacy, is today the ideal choice for those who have only time for one Mackintosh visit (p61).

Early in 1907, Mackintosh's practice (he was now Keppie's partner) was commissioned to complete the School of Art and, exactly a decade after the first phase, it was opened in December 1909. We might expect to see the architect, now aged 41, at the height of his powers, about to produce the work of his maturity. Extraordinarily, apart from a few tea rooms and one little domestic fit-out, CRM had little work again.

By 1910 Mackintosh was seen as old-fashioned. There was no new work; he became depressed and drank heavily. His strongest supporter, Fra Newbery, also became depressive and ground down by running the Art School where the less talented Keppie, as governor and then chairman, was increasingly powerful, and the new head of architecture was conspicuously pro  Franco-American and anti any Austro-Germanic influence. J J Burnet, whose role on the Art School building committee was to keep tight rein on CRM's creativity, was now building his classically ordered galleries for the British Museum in London. This was seen as the future.

In 1913, CRM failed to complete a scheme for a competition which was won by the banal entry of a junior in their office, A Graham Henderson. Henderson was soon made a partner on the strength of it, Mackintosh by that time had agreed that his partnership should end. (Henderson later became CRM's sharpest critic and the source of nasty stories about his unprofessionalism.)

By now Mackintosh was suffering from extreme depression and severe pneumonia. Giving up hope of independent architectural practice in Glasgow, in 1914 the Mackintoshes retreated to the New-

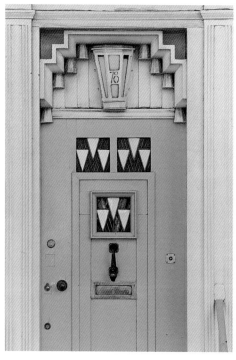

berys' holiday village in Suffolk, perhaps aiming to continue to Vienna. But once there, and with the European War breaking out, they stayed a year. In a complete break from architecture, CRM became absorbed in the most elegant and delicate botanical sketches and watercolours (over forty survive). Then, amidst the xenophobic hysteria drummed up to support the war, traumatically, CRM was picked up as a spy. Ordered out of East Anglia, the Mackintoshes escaped to the more congenial bohemian world of Chelsea, the artists' corner of London, staying for eight years.

In 1916, W J Bassett-Lowke, industrialist, model-maker and modernist, searched out CRM to convert his pokey terrace house in Northampton. Mackintosh added a shallow bay at the back; a cool, white rectangular box, facing the river to the south, which gave a touch of spaciousness to the bottom floors, framed a balcony to the main bedroom and gave a terrace to the guest room on top. But what impresses in the interior of 78 Derngate, Northampton, is the use of bold, deep colour and jagged forms amidst a shiny dark. The powerful originality of both hall and guest bedroom is clear in their recent reconstructions – the hall and stair screen for the 1996 exhibition; the bedroom in the gallery above the Mackintosh House in the Hunterian (p71).

In 1917 CRM also did one final tea room for Miss Cranston: a basement room, dug out under the Willow. CRM and MMM both designed textiles for various manufacturers (a few hundred designs survive, mostly in the Hunterian), in bright, geometric patterns, brilliant and subtle colours. The 1919 guest room at Derngate was his last built work.

In their corner of Chelsea, artist friends 'commissioned' studios, but although CRM got as far as mugging-up the LCC bye-laws, obtaining quotations for building in reinforced concrete, and submitting elevations to the ground landlord (who demanded 'more architectural qualities'), nothing came of them. The elevation to Glebe Place of three studios, a composite drawing of projects on adjoining sites designed over a year or more from early 1920, gives a hint of what a remarkable group London (and the subsequent development of British architecture before the Second World War) lost. It could have broken CRM through to a new career. But there never seems to have been the will to pursue them.

In 1920, Bassett-Lowke covered CRM's extraordinary dark hall and stair in light grey; he then asked Mackintosh to design another decorative scheme, and got a frieze in jazzy triangles and lozenges, but much lighter than before. In 1925 the frieze was used again in the Bassett-Lowkes' new, larger house, designed – because they could not track Mackintosh down – by the famous German designer, Peter Behrens.

For, the Mackintoshes had left Britain; heading for the Mediterranean, where, for four years, they lived in cheap hotels, finally stopping in Port

◀ *Mackintosh's 1916 remodelling of the door at 78 Derngate, Northampton. Bassett-Lowke had been recommended CRM. This conversion was to be Mackintosh's last architectural commission, for all later plans failed to be realised. Because of the war, Bassett-Lowke was forbidden to build a new house; but by the mid-1920s, when it was possible and he searched for the architect again, CRM could not be found at all, having abandoned both architecture and Britain.*

▶ *Mackintosh abandoned architectural practice in 1921, in his early fifties. Isolated in a Mediterranean village, in the few years he had left, CRM became a landscape watercolourist of extraordinary quality. His vision is calm and unpeopled. In* Rue du Soleil *(1926), which is in the collection of the Hunterian Art Gallery, the water is almost solid geometry; pattern and colour dominate an almost abstract composition.*

Vendres, near the Franco-Spanish border. Here, having abandoned architecture for a second and now final time, CRM concentrated on developing his watercolours towards a new vision (41 landscapes survive). Finally, illness forced Margaret back to England, soon followed by Mackintosh whose painful mouth was diagnosed as cancer. He died in December 1928, aged sixty. Margaret, never again settled or well, outlived him by just five years. On her death, all their things were valued: his drawings and everything from the studio, all their furniture including several CRM chairs and all the French paintings. The total valuation was under £90.

What was Mackintosh's position in the world of architecture? Just into the twentieth century, when in his early thirties, CRM was hailed by the Viennese Secessionists as 'our leader… who showed us the way;' and, for a German critic, in 'the list of truly original artists, the creative minds of the modern movement, the name of Charles Mackintosh would certainly be included even among the few that one can count on the fingers of a single hand.' Later, in 1913, a gathering of European architects and designers in Poland toasted: 'to our mentor Mackintosh, the greatest since the gothic.' Yet that was just when he was abandoning architectural practice, leaving Glasgow to spend the remaining years unpublished and in private obscurity. (No image of the Glasgow School of Art was published before 1924; no plan till 1950.)

For whatever reasons the Mackintosh career was not that of a successful architect. CRM-MMM worked privately and together, with little attributed to MMM alone after their marriage. Though extraordinarily talented, CRM was assistant and then partner in an ordinary architectural practice.

It is astonishing to remember, when we look back to the first decade of the century – seeing the wealth of decorative work, the great range of objects (over sixty chair designs are documented), the drawings and paintings, the remarkable interiors carved out within existing shells, and the few masterly buildings – that this man was born at the same time as Frank Lloyd Wright and only a decade before Le Corbusier, who were both building major works in the late 1950s, two generations after CRM's career had virtually ended.

Nikolaus Pevsner, the great mid twentieth cen-

tury architectural historian, researched for an essay just after Mackintosh's death. When published (much later) in English, it ended: 'He was a genius. He had a spatial imagination as fertile and complex as those of Frank Lloyd Wright and Le Corbusier… I never knew Mackintosh, but at the same time I have never met anyone – and I have approached many of his friends and contemporaries – who did not speak of him with a light in their eyes.'

GLASGOW SCHOOL OF ART

Francis Newbery, who became head while CRM was an evening student in architecture (and indeed the first Scottish student to win a Gold Medal for architecture) brought to the Glasgow School of Art an inspirational and international leadership. He wanted a new building; in 1894 his governors began to find funds and a site; by 1896 a dozen local architectural practices were invited to compete for its design. Whatever was his role in the choice of winner, Newbery and his wife Jessie became and remained Mackintosh's firm friends for life.

▶ *'Portals must have guardians', CRM read in Lethaby, the contemporary English architectural writer whose work he quoted. Here they are: the symbolic women flanking a stylised rosebush, holding the clue to the art-world of The Four. Directly over the entrance to the School of Art, as the building's literal keystone, this (1897-8) is the only ornamented stonework on the building.*

The winning scheme was designed in the second half of 1896, just two years after CRM had completed his part-time education there. Its layout, responding directly to the utilitarian brief and very tight finances, is very straightforward: a central entrance on the main lower floor climbs straight into the heart of the building. There, directly ahead, the top-lit stair leads up to the 'museum', the school's hub, next to the director's office above the entrance. Studios range to right and left on the two main floors, on the north side of long corridors; two lecture rooms, as required by the brief, are at opposite far ends, north-east corner on ground floor (which later became a studio) and south-west corner on the floor below. The land sloped steeply to the south allowing considerably more accommodation below the entrance level, although no windows were allowed on the enclosed site boundary which might be built up to by southern neighbours. The simple E-shape plan has top-lit basement studios filling the gaps in the E to the south.

At first the governors could only afford to build half; starting with the east end and central core. A decade later, when they were able to complete it, Mackintosh redesigned the west end and added a top layer of studios the length of the building, set back from the facade. The great north front, which in 1985 the US architect Robert Venturi called 'one of the greatest achievements of all time, comparable in scale and majesty to Michelangelo', was not changed.

In narrow Renfrew Street, with the rhythm of three huge studio windows one side and four the other, and the picturesque intricate composition of the central masonry element, visitors seldom realise that the entrance is precisely in the centre. The symmetrical railing and street wall add a syncopated rhythm. Subtle massing of the central form is framed by the geometry of the austere studio windows on either side, each under the great brim of their cap. It is

more than two art factories which hem in a lovable old castle. In the centre is the complex (and ambiguous) hub on top of which sits the director. Spread alongside are the mono-dimensional, focused (and clear) activities of the studios.

Look at the dynamic balance of the central composition: the oriel window to the left of the door, cut by the balcony which also separates the entrance from its formal cap, the great arch headed window. Further up, the tower stair, far taller than necessity would dictate, rises to the director's private (recessed, shady) studio. To the sides, the studio rhythm is detailed with rolled masonry edges to the great windows hitting their sharply cut, recessed but expressed steel lintels. (Note the one tiny window between two great studios; it lights a model's changing space.) The rest of the metalwork we can see here humanises surfaces, articulates silhouette and edges, and enriches with metaphor: the delicate iron brackets with their individual flowery open knots in front of the plain window framing; the finials atop the towers; the individual symbolic discs on the street edge rising from their clumps of wrought-iron tulips. Perhaps it is important we are not told all their meanings.

Before entering, look at the building flanks. The east wall in Dalhousie Street remains from the 1890s, an asymmetrical composition with obviously picturesque baronial touches. The right half, being the side wall of the studios, naturally, is blank (windows beside the basement door are later changes). On the left, the scale changes dramatically as it runs steeply down hill, here with its own symmetry of bow windows (for the board room) over the heavy rounded pediment of the staff room double window.

Walking to the other side, there is no clue on the great north front that, beyond the front steps, this half face is a decade newer; nor can the additional floor of studios, set back from the edge, be seen from the pavement. Then we turn the corner into Scott Street.

Now the decade's development seems more like a century removed from the eastern end. The great blank, uncoursed wall of dressed rubble with its one romantic, tiny window, flanking the studios, remembers its ancient cousin, the opposite bookend in Dalhousie Street. But now, layered onto this, is new masonry work formed with the sharp skill CRM had recently honed at Scotland Street School, here used with fearless incisiveness. Six identically cut ground-floor bays march across this wall; and from the southern three, oriels soar up, 62 ft (19 m) to their triangular gable. All this is

▶ *The astonishing vertical sweep of the great library windows at the south-west corner of the School of Art (1907-8), outlined in crisply detailed and geometrically sharp masonry frames. To the right, on the south flank, the window forms are sunk into the harled surface.*

articulated in carefully coursed ashlar, held in an utterly precise geometry of solid articulated bays of stratified glass, masked with the small square net of bronze framing (which replaced the original iron in 1947) and masonry courses. In the centre are the three great library windows, with half-cylinders of masonry flanking them, intended for never-executed sculptures. Down the hill, looking round the corner to the south, the west block is built up to the property line over which no projections were allowed. So while the west is modelled beyond the wall-plane, on the south it is all within the plane. Here the articulated bays repeat, the symmetrical composition responding to that round the corner, but now sunk as if disappearing into the harled surface's quicksand.

Before leaving the west end, as we climb back past the sub-basement screen and iron gateway, look at the strange basement level door on Scott Street; so staggered and layered, with its Mannerist reversals as always in CRM's formal playing, like the shadowy keystone. If we did not know, we might wonder when it was built; and, more interesting than calling it 'proto Deco' and so on, wonder why it was built? What did CRM mean by all this layering of planes and lines? It certainly worried the governors' sense of financial economy when, on a site visit with only the basement built, they looked uncomprehendingly at its complexity!

Robert Venturi's comparison with Michelangelo is not hyperbole. In his 1968 book *Complexity and Contradiction in Architecture*, Venturi was the first author after the era of Modernism to deal with the great Mannerist architects, from Michelangelo to Hawksmoor to Lutyens. Mackintosh, in forming the skin of this west block, now had a fluent command of his language; in his reversals of the rules, hinted at in earlier projects, in the final phase of the School of Art he is playing in this company.

To enter, we must climb back to Renfrew Street. Up the tightening steps enclosed by curving walls and under the great knot – the symbolic women flanking a stylised rose bush as the building's literal key stone – which is the building's only ornamented stonework. Directly beneath stands one dead central timber column. At first the porch was open (which makes sense of the janitor's enquiry hatch on the left). When doors had to be added, right at the top of the steps, (they not only say 'art' and 'school' in CRM's inimitable fingerprint, but also 'in' and 'out', to avoid awful accidents), he hung onto the column's importance by hanging the doors from it, rather than from the sides as we might expect. Entering these narrowest of actual doors, what an astonishing change of scale is forced by this compression! (Note the squares of glass of the hatch to the left and three bright blue, welcoming glass hearts in the inner door frames ahead.) Then the odd different symmetry of the entrance hall is suddenly revealed, tightly held among solid, squat columns under a crypt's low vault. The pillars to the left become revealed as central in a double space, widened into a pausing place, and now opening into the shop. Today, guided tours start here and my description follows the usual route.

Straight ahead, the stairs rise to the light of the school's central exhibition space. Here, in this steel and concrete building, is a timber cage of overlap-

▶ *Approaching the door to the Headmaster's office (or director, as we say today), showing how CRM (in 1898-9) touches the dour, 'plain building' (as was required by his client body) with details of great charm at the points to which our eyes and bodies come close. (Every door at the School of Art is worth noticing; see also p72.)*

ping square balustrading and tall newels, some coming right up from the basement floor, others continuing up to the roof trusses flanking the stairwell. As we rise, and our eyes look further up, we see it is covered with almost barn-like wooden trusses softened by little hearts, inspired by Voysey, cut into their posts. Those round the stair are carried on the timber columns; however, those to the sides have column caps simply floating in the

space. Thus Mackintosh's mannerist games continue. (Note on the stair, by the way, Glasgow's coat of arms, the remarkable iron rod abstraction of a tree which supports rather more literal bell, bird and fish.)

To the north, the director has a dark threshold across which, unfortunately, you probably will not be invited into his private sanctum today. If you manage to penetrate for a moment, it is well worth it. The door opens into another world: bright yet enclosed. In here the cornice both holds the pure cube of the room, tying in the lovely concealed stair to his private studio above, plus storage and a WC, and breaks it, flowing gently into the deep window bay, its vault seeming scooped out of the thickness of the wall, like a castle window's deep embrasure.

Moving along the corridor to the east, look up at the shapes made by the bellying cuts of the light-wells in the black-framed ceiling under the lean-to roof-lights beyond. If possible (and other than at diploma show time it may not be), look in to the left, at one of the great, working studios; direct, industrially formed machines for capturing and diffusing light. (These nearly 33 ft (10 m) tall spaces, with 8 ft (2.5 m) wide hidden, flat roof-lights, have from the start had hot air central heating.) The lower 10 ft (3 m) of the dividing cross-walls between these studios used to be removable: what an astonishing layered, horizontal space that must have been with them stacked away.

There was originally only the central stair, and when escape stairs were required at either wing, one enclosed the board room's west-facing bay windows. It is said the board refused to use this room; and certainly before 1909, when the stair wrapped it, this was a design studio. In 1947 it became 'The Mackintosh Room'. This is not a Mackintosh setting; but in here is a variety of CRM furniture, chairs from the range of tea rooms and, among other artifacts, one of MMM's finest gesso panels, *The Heart of the Rose*. Note the light fittings (particularly the magnificent central one) which all came from Windyhill. Also from that house came perhaps the most impressive object: the long, dark bookcase. Hanging on the wall alongside is an earlier drawing for a toy-chest (note the side shelves below for 'hammers tools etc' and the end doors above to hide books). Being too massive for the Davidsons' playroom, it was redesigned with considerably more elegance (for which the final drawing was given to the Art School by Tom Howarth). It is a wonderful, if scarcely domestic, object; its four leaded rose

▶ *The tiniest Mackintosh detail is handled with a charm and appropriateness; neither overdone nor thrown away. The slightly projecting, identical cement squares on every half-landing of the east and west stairs each contain a different number of differently coloured 3 in square (70 mm) glazed tiles.*

panels (see p9) like the brilliant designs on an out-stretched black silk kimono.

The stair, which just misses those bay windows, giving us a tiny theatrical frisson of outside / inside ambiguity, rises to the top studios. On the barest, almost medieval walls with their grey polished plaster, little squares of square coloured tiles attract the eye and fingers at each half-landing; every one is different. It is again the mix of sturdiness and delicacy, which CRM handles with unrivalled sureness – just like the tiny eyes of coloured leaded glass in the black doors and their rough corridors. And then at the top, reminding us that this stair was designed after those at Scotland Street (p58), we reach the portcullis, where a cage of metal flats under a circle veils the junction of masonry with timber roof. A

dark dungeon in the air, before we move along and out to the dramatic opposite extreme: the fragile, perilous passageway in the sky.

To link east and west when this additional top floor was added, Mackintosh didn't break into the existing central tower (the director's studio). Instead he cantilevered a walkway (always known as the 'hen-run') off its south wall, a light timber net enclosed only in glass.

This fragile passage leads to a vaulted loggia, whose bays offer the best view in Glasgow,

beyond Alexander Thomson's St Vincent Street Church and away to the south. There is no better place, in any building in Britain, for students to sit quietly working or to loiter – were it not the threshold to the professors' private studios! Before descending, stick your nose if at all possible into the studio straight ahead at the end of the loggia (room 58). This is the Composition Room above the library; the one studio with a south window, which also has, hanging off its south-east corner, the extraordinary little conservatory you saw from the loggia, for the precision plant studies at which CRM himself so excelled. To look at the tiniest of plants in the brightest light, high in the sky, was a touch of pure romance. (This conservatory appears on the very first, otherwise exceedingly plain south elevation, the competition drawing of 1896.) Note this studio's freestanding columns (steel) and beams (timber) with their spare Japanese austerity, the geometry of the three low cuts in the gable and see how the bays, so prominent up to the cornice on the outside, become solid masonry inside.

Down half a storey, the former book store above the library now shows off a Mackintosh furniture collection. It was not designed as a pleasant public space. But, while admiring its contents, enjoy the room's qualities too: look out of the windows, and especially down into the library oriels. Note also the ingenious structure: the floor (which is the library ceiling) is suspended from the low steel beams by eight pairs of twisted straps.

The west stair continues down to the library, and through its leaded glass doors, into the sacred grove of knowledge. The forest clearing, its trees silhouetted against the brightness beyond; the grouped lamps hanging on chains from darkness, with their jangling detail, folded structures of black and silver, hole-punched, metal flats around naked light bulbs, abstract, exotic birds with their touches of blue and pink glass, their dazzle veiling the dark canopy above. Never can the arrival at this moment

◀ *Spatially, the library (1909) is Mackintosh's tour-de-force. Complex, intricate and yet intimate, it is extraordinarily difficult to contain in a photograph. Carrying the narrow gallery across the tall windows, which fly up past yet another storey, was controversial from the start. In January 1909 the client committee objected that it would jeopardise the interior light. However, at a committee meeting which its architect members (led by J J Burnet) were unable to attend, CRM cheekily argued that it would be too expensive at this late stage in the process to change the design by removing it. Mackintosh won his balcony.*

27

of electricity in architecture have been better cele-
brated than in these fittings from 1909.

The central clearing is formed by eight wide
trees, whose thick lower trunks are made up of
three pieces; the outer two branch back to support the gallery, while the central trunk continues
up, joining other thinner verticals from the gallery,
to the forest canopy of crisscrossed branches.
Underneath such metaphors, just as under the
decorated, scalloped almost frilled surfaces,
the interior spatial geometry is precisely controlled
and clearly articulated. And the structure all ties
together; the columns standing on great steel
joists in the floor just touch the ceiling, each being
tied up to the twisted hangers from the higher
steels we saw in the room above.

If you know this space from photographs, its
intimate scale can be a shock. (It is only 36 ft
(11 m) square.) Note the central table, with five
perforated and carved uprights at each end; the
screen and periodical rack with its tiny glass inserts
at the top was wrapped round it some years later
by CRM. Similar decoration appears on the laths of
the gallery front, where you will see that no two
combinations of holes are identical.

On three sides the gallery sits on cranked
beams, back from the supporting columns; but
CRM's boldest move was to carry it across the
windows. Unfortunately, with its narrow stair and
limited space above, this area cannot be accessible
to visitors. But move under it.

The spaces formed between the worlds of
inside and out are always among the most telling
in CRM's work, but this transitional place is excep-
tional. You cannot walk into it, but poke your
head in and look up; sense the elements and
enclosure and the gallery reverse bays which
create extraordinary hexagonal columns of space
rising above you.

We finally must mention the board room,
though it is not usually open to the public. Here

▶ *Mackintosh
designed many
clock faces, each
appropriate to its
purpose (there
are very different
ones on p38 and
p68; also in
The School of
Art, in the
director's room,
is a beautiful
standing clock
from the Willow
Tea Rooms). This
face is one of a
group of similar
but not all iden-
tical electric wall
clocks, mounted
in public places
round the school
and controlled
from a master.*

in 1906, the board who so disliked their original tall white space, found a new, stuffy, classical home, carved out of a ground floor studio. Dark and enclosed, it is a most unusual room. (Look up at the ceiling, a heavy mesh of layers of structure, and at the three extraordinary clusters of hammered copper light fittings in delicate wrought iron, under it.) Certainly there never have been Ionic capitals like the eight, each different, here.

Was this space Mackintosh's ironic comment on the new classical orthodoxy of Edwardian academic architecture by the time the building was finished? Much of the unhappiness in the story of CRM and the School of Art can be read from Newbery's group portrait of governors which hangs in this room: the architect was added on an additional strip of canvas at the left after the portrait had been approved. His expression is honestly captured.

This building began as Mackintosh's masterpiece, in the old sense of the piece which ends an apprenticeship, honours mastery of the skill, and heralds a mature career. It gained him his partnership, after all. And it ends as his masterpiece, in the modern sense, because it developed after the seven-year gap of CRM's confident career, into something quite different. It is also his masterpiece, as we so easily see in retrospect, because there simply weren't any others which followed.

CHURCHES

Mackintosh's one church is St Matthew's Free Church, at Queen's Cross, north-west of central Glasgow. Having become redundant, it was taken over by the Charles Rennie Mackintosh Society whose headquarters it has been since 1977. Early in 1897 he designed this building at the junction of two main roads, Garscube and Maryhill, on Glasgow's northern edge. Its picturesque image in a simple, gothic revival form is dominated by the tapering and cut off corner tower, directly based on a real medieval one which had been sketched by Mackintosh in Somerset a year or two earlier. The turret (precisely copied from the English church, and an extravagant flourish here to house a simple gallery stair) grows from its side, and rises to a lookout.

On the main road, there are four quite different groups of bays: a high pair, a low pair and the end ones each with a door. Below a tracery window in the corner tower is the main entrance; in the porch tower at the eastern end – and under a peculiar and beautifully carved column which splits the window overhead – is the minor entrance. Today both are closed. To get in, you must walk round the corner into Springbank Street, passing below the large art-nouveau-gothic window, to the vestry door where the bell is answered by the CRM Society during opening hours.

The masonry forms and details are full of imaginative play, but once inside we see that it is more than just decorative surface. The two entrances, we now realise, do not come directly into the church but enter vestibules from which, turning right or left, we either go up to a gallery or enter the side of this large, barn-like preaching hall, in an ambiguous aisle underneath its side gallery.

If its simplicity pleased the Free Church, its unexpected asymmetry added a dynamism to that

◀ *Looking from the back gallery across Queen's Cross Church (1897), the slight asymmetries are made clear in this axial view: the west window does not quite align with the lamp over the chancel entrance, the communion table and the not-quite-central aisle. The building's major asymmetry, however, just out of shot to the left, is the side gallery, which juts into the nave from its own space beyond the barrel vault.*

essentially static space. The side gallery beyond the main roof, under its own two gabled bays and bearing little obvious relation to the church's interior space, is said to derive from a Japanese inn which Mackintosh knew from a book.

The details in the church interior, which is now restored to good condition, are full of invention. From the beautifully (and strangely) carved pulpit, past the lamp over the centre of the chancel

Detail of the Queen's Cross Church pulpit carving; with abstracted bird and botanical imagery closely relating to CRM's symbolic painting of the mid 1890s.

entrance, our eyes wander upwards and unexpectedly meet the rivets on the great plated steel beams tying the upturned keel overhead. 'The arching of the roof, with enormous rafters stretching across it, possessed my fancy with ideas of Noah's Ark,' said Mackintosh, about the 'Basilica' which he had earlier visited in Vicenza, in Italy. He hadn't forgotten.

If not a great building, it is far from the conventional 1890s solution to the given architectural problem, full of quirky and often fascinating spatial as well as decorative detail. Look at the pendants in the gallery balustrade (and the capitals below), a motif CRM would develop to maturity in the Art School library over a decade later. Even if not stopping for a cup of tea, note the trusses in the roof-lit hall.

The next year, Mackintosh designed a Mission Hall in Ruchill Street, again for the Free Church. A short walk west along Maryhill Road from Queen's Cross, it stands – in grey rather than red sandstone – now rather lonely in the desert of Glasgow's destroyed street architecture. It is a small building, with interesting if simple shapes on the façade (eyebrows and nose surround windows to the right of the door). The main hall is top lit, which focuses on the elaborate cross beams.

Having not been appointed to design the adjoining church, which followed three years later, Mackintosh never built another church. Although he did design elements inside at least two others; a pulpit, a communion table, an organ case, light fittings and other decoration for a church near Stirling in 1904 and also for another (in 1905-6), which has since been demolished, in Paisley to the south-west of Glasgow.

Door detail at Queen's Cross Church

WINDYHILL

Although there are no genuine CRM houses in Glasgow, there are two real ones within commuting distance down the Clyde. To the south is Windyhill, at Kilmacolm in Renfrewshire. Please note that this is a private residence with no public access. To the north of the broad Firth of Clyde, in Helensburgh, and still easily accessible from

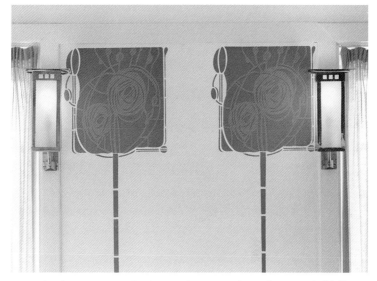

central Glasgow by suburban railway, is The Hill House.

Windyhill (1899-1901) might be seen as a step on the path to the considerably larger Hill House, built a few years later, at over twice the cost. It remains, however, an extraordinary achievement itself. Windyhill is Mackintosh's first essay in the sculptural massing of forms within a vernacular tradition, all unified (and dematerialised) under a cover of harling – Scottish rough-cast. More important is the beautiful refined calm in its interiors, not overwhelmed with the 'rose boudoir' decoration of earlier Mackintosh interiors.

At Windyhill we see CRM's separate worlds of outside and in. The vernacular, unassuming and traditional exterior seen from the gate (1899), and the modern, artistic and delicate interior in the bedroom (1901).

HOUSE FOR AN ART LOVER

The House for an Art Lover, of course, was not a real commission, but an ideas competition, set by the interior design magazine *Zeitschrift fur Innendekoration*, which the Mackintoshes entered in a hurry in 1901. Though they didn't win (perhaps because their entry was incomplete), the set of drawings was published by the competition sponsor in 1902 as beautifully produced and subtly coloured lithographic plates.

The building completed nearly a century later in Bellahouston park is not a Mackintosh work. Inspired by the original drawings of CRM, it was realised by John Kane and Graeme Robertson (up to 1990), under Andrew MacMillan. It operates as an international graduate study centre for the Glasgow School of Art, a conference and function centre, high quality café and design shop.

The competition brief dictated the main spaces and also their size. Internally, we have here a memory of Windyhill, with touches of The Hill House (though that was designed later), writ luxurious and oh so large within an historic country house form. If you know the stair at The Hill House, the one in the hall here is like a giant's version – although the overall size is not that much more; all the details seem quite overscaled. Interestingly Roger Billcliffe has questioned if CRM would ever have wanted to build a house on this scale. The sadness is not that he didn't build this, but that its successful publication, known across Europe and in the USA, didn't lead to any other real architectural commissions.

The cavernous north-facing hall, with its low, enclosed gallery where facsimiles of CRM's published drawings are now displayed on a lectern, leads, through simple sliding doors, to the vaulted, comparatively low, but still overscaled dining room. This severe space, with its simple, strong-grained oak and its stone fireplace (virtually that in the Art School's first board room) is, like all the public rooms, well crafted. Many of the details are beautifully recreated: fireplace, furniture, lights and decorative panels, all in the forms of a Mackintosh country house.

The Ladies' Room is elegant and intimate. Right next door is the spectacular, long music and reception room. Still lacking the promised panels by MMM in every window bay and each side of the

piano at the end, indeed with the constructed piano no less extraordinary but considerably less ornamented than as drawn by CRM, the richness does not dazzle, though the space may overwhelm.

What must impress here, more than spatial ingenuity, is surface decoration, detail and elaboration. To a visitor, therefore, it feels not unlike a visit to a stately home: except there is something peculiarly nouveau here; fleeting senses of Disney cannot easily be avoided. Cecil Beaton would have used these spaces as sets for 'My Fair Lady'. Glasgow's new image of itself would love nothing better. In its first months of opening, it was already selling itself in 1997 as a key attraction and one of the city's most popular venues.

The House for an Art Lover, built 1989-96 based on CRM's (1900-1) competition sketches, and within its own garden in Bellahouston Park.

THE HILL HOUSE

The Hill House is Mackintosh's domestic master-piece, now in the care of the National Trust for Scotland. It is a fair walk from the seafront up the hill to the plot which his client bought in 1902, five minutes above the upper station from Glasgow, and among the prosperous mansions of Upper Helensburgh. Almost next door, there already was an Arts & Crafts house by Baillie Scott (who had won a prize in the Art Lover's House competition); nearby were others by more local architects but mostly appearing equally English – with foreign whitewash, half-timbering and lots of red-tile roofs. The client 'put to Mackintosh such ideas as I had for my prospective dwelling. I told him that I disliked red-tiled roofs in the West of Scotland with its frequent murky sky; did not want to have a construction of brick and plaster and wooden beams; that, on the whole, I rather fancied grey rough cast for the walls, and slate for the roof; and any architectural effect sought should be secured by the massing of the parts rather than by adventitious ornamentation. To all these sentiments Mackintosh at once agreed... My wife and I were shown over a house he'd designed at Kilmacolm, and left convinced that Mackintosh was the man for us.'

The house recalls the Scots 'baronial', in outside image and even more in plan; but we need not chase its origins in a fusion of the conventional Edwardian north-corridor house (the west half), and a seventeenth-century Z-plan Scots tower-house (to the east). Simply approach this stately, solid house, clearly rooted in its place; knock at the dark door, absolutely plain apart from a square of nine small square lenses of clear glass; and enter.

Through an inner screen that is really a glazed thick trellis, and before rising four steps into the main hall, to the right is the door of the library. This is the client, Walter Blackie's study, lined with

◀ *The hall of The Hill House with clock, chair, carpet and light fitting designed for it in 1903-4. Influences from Japanese archi-tecture to a classical Greek frieze are sub-sumed into a quintessential Mackintosh interior space.*

dark stained, grainy oak bookshelves and simple, rather Arts & Crafts, detailing; note the metal butterfly drawer-pulls. But the door's four, long, purple inserts of sparkling handmade glass had already intimated a less than conventional room beyond; and sure enough CRM offsets the conservative order with tiny inlaid squares of white enamel and purply-blue coloured glass, broken into by an occasional, single curving reed climbing the bookcase. This tall room is kept low by the oak fittings whose surrounding top rail at 8 ft (2.5 m) links together fireplace with its little windows, door and all the bookcases between. Then the southern window bursts upwards through this frieze, just like CRM's own studio at home. Mr Blackie would receive visitors here; it is the last of the world outside; only family and close friends penetrate further.

Looking up the four steps into the hall gives the feeling that we are still outside, in the public realm of getting and spending; that there is another threshold to be crossed before arrival at the heart. The progression deeper from the dark entrance towards the softest white at the house's heart centres on this hall and stair, on those intermediate spaces between the black and white. Once again CRM holds two extremes in dynamic equilibrium: one is seen in the hard shell, characterised by the adjectives strong, sober, empiricist, objective; here as at Scotland Street School, Windyhill, or even the School of Art, it is essentially a variant on the vernacular, on tradition. At the other end is the white interior, which attracts adjectives such as soft, decorated, idealist, fantastic, erotic; and this is essentially creative and modern – as in the School of Art director's room or the Mackintoshes' own living space. Here at The Hill House the actual outside shows one extreme; the deepest interior space, the master bedroom, the other. Of the other main rooms, the library tends to the dark (more traditional in its finishes and its decoration

▶ Baronial elements at The Hill House (1902) belie a very different interior. CRM proposed a square garden divided into nine squares, but this never materialised. Mackintosh's only traces on the landscape are in the semi-circle up to the door, and the balancing rose-garden on the opposite side. As you circle the house, wonder at the changing satisfaction of its form, every view offering delightful, asymmetrical but tightly controlled compositions.

as well as more sober); the drawing room tends to the light. Halls and stair mediate between the masculine, rather dour, tradition-conscious public world, and the feminine, almost dreamlike, fantastic and freely creative private world.

The lower hall appears ahead as a palely lit clearing in the dark forest through which we now approach. Note to the left, between the dark verticals, a shadowy hidden seat (under the upper

stair) from which we could be observed entering. Moving forward, solid and void uprights divide the dynamic space; tiny flashes of pink glass embedded in wood pass the eye. Turn left to climb; first four more steps and then turn the other way into the cool, north-lit stair drum. We run our hands across the open hall timbers as we do forest trees, not as the sensual sculpture in the white room ahead. These are structure: strong, expressive, dark beams and posts and planks for stair ballisters. Though explicit and constructive, this is no Arts & Crafts exercise in honest carpentry; it is symbolic rather than vernacular.

Through the frame at the head of the stair, six

little squares of glowing leaded glass in the dark door invite us into the Blackies' bedroom. Indeed all round the house tiny accents are made by touches of colour, of glass, of ceramic, of mosaic; used like lipstick or ear-rings, only in the places you are close enough to touch. The door opens and we enter an ivory mist. (Not only is the other side of the dark door now white, but its little glass squares are enamelled pink inside.) Here materiality is disguised; wooden furniture is abstractly curvaceous, smoothly feminine and thickly lacquered in an ivory white – an extreme contrast to the structural clarity of stained timber in the library. The bedroom has an overall sleekness. With the material and carpentry obscured in the absence of a workman's touch, it is all sensual surface – curves, sharpness and extreme subtlety of form.

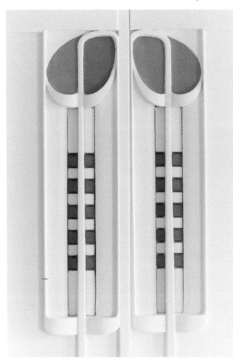

Note, however, how precisely the room is formed. The bed recess is beautifully contained under a low barrel ceiling. The shallow, enclosing vault springs from wardrobe doors on one side and from a gentle bow, echoing the vault itself, on the other. This bedside space bellies out to one tiny, low window at its centre. Here the whole thickness of the protective bedroom wall seems scooped dangerously thin; it is a riskily exposed moment in this womb-like, enclosing place. Safely thick little curving, interior shutters, each with three milky pink glass squares in them, when opened admit the morning sun to hit the pillow.

Mackintosh intended this intimate vault to be separated by gossamer veils edged with bejewelled glazed screens. That would leave two spaces; first, the dressing area: under the light fitting and in front of the tall mirror between the two windows. The symmetry of the mirror between the windows is balanced by a tall, ladder-back black chair between the twin wardrobes, which appear to reflect the window forms as negative solids of space. The second space, the fireside ingle, links to this, held by the enclosing band formed by the line of light fitment, window-head and wardrobe-tops. Here the built-in settle opposite the washstand snuggles into the wall thickness, the seat's top aligning with the fireplace.

Onto all this geometric order, built up of cubes and the two shallow cylindrical curves, a veil of decoration is layered. All the ivory walls are most delicately stencilled as a rose bower in mauve and green; between the wardrobes the roses climb through the black grid of that trellis-backed chair. This frieze is uninhibited and light, in contrast to the more polite and formal beauty we will see in the drawing room below. Flower heads fly, and long leaves blow like hair in the wind. Here is a nudity not of masculine structure, as in the stair hall, but of sensual feminine surface.

The strangely curved, smooth, ivory-lacquered shapes set off the naturally coloured materials – the pewter water jug, untreated fabrics, mirror, or enamel and pinkish tiles, the extraordinary, sharp luxuriousness of naked, polished sheet-steel with inlaid mosaic roses around the fire. In this deepest interior of the house, all hint of historical reference or vernacular has vanished. The freshness and yet sensuality is very far from its contemporary, the cloying, entwining continental art nouveau (p6).

Before leaving, note the small white table. It is

◄ _In the principal bedroom, two ivory wardrobes flank an austere black ladderback chair which stands in front of a frieze of informal roses stencilled on the wall. This balance of geometric and organic is seen in detail on the double doors of each wardrobe. Elegant botanical abstraction against patterns of squares, all in milky pink glass and layers of thick lacquered cream paint. (Not being allowed to touch, we must take on trust the stunning visual effect of looking through these doors when open against the sunlight.)_

square topped, with four legs more like leaves than stems, paper thin but curving down, facing each other diagonally, and joined by a little square timber with four square holes cut from it; that geometric description belies the extreme elegance of this delicate, dynamic and satisfying object. Leaving the bedroom, we are gently squeezed by the narrowing of the ogee curved door jambs, out of which are cut little rectangular niches for a flower vase at face level.

Glance next door, into the one other sober, masculine space (where the dark woods and simple purple highlights are in a similar language to the library). This is Walter Blackie's dressing room at the top of the stairs; then, next to it, note the wash room with its wonderful shower, perhaps the first such shower in Scotland, where horizontal jets spurt from a cage of chromed copper pipes. In the dressing room don't miss the exquisitely simple mirror in front of the window; the square in which Blackie framed his face and his day's first thoughts, the open rectangles to the sides framing the Arts & Crafts red-roofed neighbour. Also, note how CRM wraps, with an explicitness and quiet irony, a heavy mahogany wardrobe round Blackie's antique chest of drawers.

In the upper hall note the inglenook, the little 'seat-room', up two steps, low ceiled, and enclosed with arms, as if in the thickness of the wall. Anne Ellis (the National Trust's custodian) calls this alcove a 'sit-ooterie', after the half-secret spaces where a girl could safely sit out a dance but yet remain on the edge of the ballroom floor. The Hill House has many such rooms within rooms, or rather such edge places, half in and half out of rooms, which revel in the playfulness of such ambiguity. They are natural spaces for children, who so instinctively enjoy these boundary games as well as the changes of scale.

In the second bedroom opposite, look at the drawings originally deposited with the Dean of

▶ *The stairlight is built of a structure of nine cubes. The four corner cubes of this open-work metal cage, which contain the light bulbs, are each glazed on all four sides with a cube of nine little leaded glass squares. It is one of CRM's most remarkable forms, not least in that we can only see it by spiralling round it as we descend, from looking down on it to its being right above us.*

Guild for building permission, now exhibited (in facsimile). Note on plan how the billiard room would have been, and how the drawing room music bay has changed; and how, further along this corridor are other bedrooms and the hidden ways up to the wonderful children's world. (We can only imagine the effect of its glorious window when looking up from outside, unless we hire it for a holiday flat from The Landmark Trust).

Much of the house was finished and filled quite conventionally; and more bedrooms have recently been opened to the public. But Blackie gave CRM complete control of library, main bedroom, drawing room and hallways, including cabinets and cases, chairs and clocks, carpets  and wall decoration. A large proportion of this is carefully in place (often restored or, like carpets, replaced) today.

On the way back downstairs, note the stair light, another of CRM's most remarkable objects; it epitomises his geometric concerns at The Hill House – and it can only be seen by moving diagonally past. At first it is below eye-level, its form revealing itself as we spiral down underneath it. Down into the hall, we are surrounded by Mackintosh's metamorphosis of a classic frieze, the triglyphs and metopes of the Greek temple. The expressive metopes are here squares of pale blue stencilling, with pink and black checkerboard patterns and one carefully placed touch of green. The triglyphs between, articulated strictly geometrically, framed in dark oak, are sets of three tall thin strips of pale purple enamelled glass. Its essence is a balance between the extremes emphasised in the rooms we have already seen, these opposites of tradition and modernity, dark and light, nature and artifice, masculine and feminine, yin and yang.

From this evenly north-lit platform, a dark door with six glowing little opal white squares opens to the most brilliant distant view: every visitor must draw breath on opening this door. Directly ahead, a glazed rectangular bay, diminutive under a lowered ceiling which acts as the brim of a cap, captures the stunning panorama across the distant water of the Firth of Clyde to the south.

As ever Mackintosh's strictly geometric armature here carves three-dimensional spaces with precision. To the left another small rectangle is cut in the wall. Darker than the window space ahead, and similarly separated by the horizontal planes, this space is for music. The room, therefore, is graduated from the winter fireside to the garden, via the music alcove, which with its own little window and window seat is also a tiny room within a room. The window bay is a bower, slightly mysteriously enveloping as we approach. It is surprisingly deep, a real little sum-

Detail of the wall stencilling in the drawing room, a more formalised wrapping than in the bedroom, based on patterns of seven squares among the abstracted roses.

mer room, with its own threshold layers: through the wall thickness, across the light strip, to reach the little columns which define the seat space. There is a sense of fragility, of vulnerability, stepping into this space – we have broken through the great solid harled mansion wall, we find glass down to our feet on both sides – and yet we are safely held close. Note the delicate white columns, opening into stylised flower petals at the head,

which frame the seat; little geometric panels of pink and green leaded glass, across which bends a single blue-ish reed, are high on the white panelling, pink leaded glass inset in the ceiling above.

The main rectangle of the room is held within a light, encircling band unified by a low cornice which forms the door and fireplace head and the ceiling height of the music alcove and the window bay. Below, a trellis of white and shiny silvery stripes decorated with pink roses, pale green foliage, and occasional falling petals, catches and throws the light differently as we move. Above, the space rises another metre; the shape, disappearing into darkness, is ambiguous, for both

The music 'room' and the window 'room' extend beyond the drawing room. When CRM was asked to replace his ceiling mounted lights in this room he fitted the lower wall sconces which remain.

47

walls and ceiling are the same deep damson. (At least it should be; when the wall lights replaced gas fittings which had dropped from the white ceiling to the rail height, CRM finally specified a dark, low-gloss 'plum' sheen. Having been painted a dead black for many years it is currently 'restored' to CRM's first, pale proposal – though the original drop gas lights are not reinstated. Where, as here, we know of various extremely different decorative

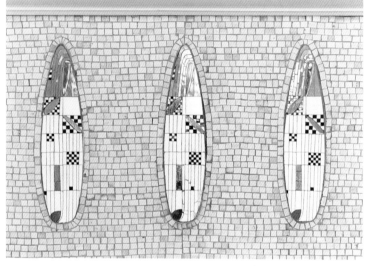

Detail of drawing room fireplace mosaic.

schemes by CRM, conservation proposals become an unusually interesting topic for argument!)

The slightly concave fireplace, with its mosaic surround and oval mirror inserts behind the fire irons, holds a fine gesso panel by MMM. Note the shelving unit to the fire's left, with its central plant and branching pink glass leaves at each shelf; and look at the window opposite, whose edges are ever so slightly curved into the room, with seven little pink glass squares and a longer slit beneath, mediating between light and dark.

All the movable furniture, like the beautiful cabinet at the end, between this window and the fire, is dark, stained or ebonised. (This cabinet repays close inspection. See how the glass doors are subtly curved and angled; note also the little decorative triangles in the centre below these doors, the motif, also used at the same moment on Scotland Street school, which so dominated CRM's later pattern-making.) In counter-point to the little table we saw in the bedroom, a small black table stands in front of the bay. This key piece, made for the room in May 1908, is a geometrically pure essay in squares. Its formal austerity is melted, as ever: the centre of the top has four mother-of-pearl inlaid squares, each of which actually consists of nine tiny squares, set with their grains at right angles to each other, thus catching the light differently as we move past. Just as the white table in the bedroom was not entirely feminine, but softened from a conceptual, formal armature, so here, the rigorous, abstract, black geometry, is centred on this delicate, feminine, natural patina, its surface fleeting with our changing viewpoint.

Before leaving, see the very different dark, panelled dining room, where Mackintosh incorporated the Blackies' traditional Edwardian values. Antique furniture and silver stands alongside CRM's sober bronze and white glass shapes on the window-wall and magnificent gas light fitting over the table, where deep purple encloses a white glass interior.

Notice how CRM's yin and yang of composition, material and form, has been intimated almost subliminally, in the stencil pattern just inside the front door. On the threshold between the public and private worlds, the porch decoration is a very simple stencil: the shadow of a flower curves across a checkerboard ground, (we see the proportion 5:8:13 which, in Fibonacci's series, tends towards golden section). It sums up Mackintosh's desired dynamic balance. His aim was the nurturing of a modern life, which could be protected within society by a strong, masculine shield; one whose goal, within this nurturing eggshell, was 'sweetness, simplicity, freedom, confidence and light.'

TEA ROOMS

Catherine Cranston more or less invented the Glasgow tea room phenomenon. She filled the need for a miniature social centre which served many purposes: to be a safe meeting place for bourgeois men in a city famed for the evils wrought by drink; but more, it uniquely offered 'ladies rooms' where respectable women could got out and meet, at a time – a century ago – when women without men in the urban scene were usually taken for servants or prostitutes. These were not cafés, but offered a range of privacies in the public world; rooms for lunch or private dining, rooms to read and write, to play billiards or smoke. They were almost clubs without bedrooms; and, centrally of course, without alcohol. Kate Cranston had avant-garde taste, and became the Mackintoshes' most stalwart patron.

Though CRM had earlier done a mural for Buchanan Street and furniture for Argyle Street, the Ladies' Luncheon Room for Cranston's temple to temperance in Ingram Street was, in 1900, the Mackintoshes' first complete tea room interior. Designed for the (16 ft 6 in / 5 m high) ground floor space in Miss Cranston's block, it was rebuilt for the Mackintosh exhibition in 1996.

The end bay held the silver-walled entrance corridor and stair; a low screen in which are set glazed panels separates this entrance from the lunch room where, once seated, over the lobby we see the great curvaceous panel (14 ft 9 in / 4.5 m long) entitled *The Wassail*. This is CRM's work, and parallel, on the opposite side wall appeared its partner, MMM's *May Queen*. Both these vast artworks went to the Vienna exhibition of 1900.

On the other sides were a back gallery and, opposite it, the window wall which was handled as a space of its own. Double depths of column at the street, with a high-level rail binding the inner columns, marked each window bay as an

◀ *The last and most remarkable Cranston tea room was The Willow. Here the most complete space is the Room de Luxe (1903). The room is encircled by a deep band of dissolving complexity at eye height. The long side is a range of windows, each inset with silver mirrored hearts (seen from outside on p53). The other sides are ranges of mirror inset with panes leaded in purple and pink glass. (Silver chair backs with inset pink glass squares can be seen mirrored in this image.)*

individual place, with its own banquette seat and facing black, tall-backed chairs.

As restored for the exhibition, in 1996, we notice how the screen – the alternating leaded glass panels below, of pure, abstract vegetable designs simply in translucent pale pea, black and white – doesn't fight with the extraordinary richness above – vast panels of gesso on hessian and scrim, the bejewelled and beflowered ladies formed with twine, glass beads, thread, mother-of-pearl and tin leaf. Between them, little drop-lights, so simple and yet so beautiful, give a golden down-glow reflected in the saucer above and the fireworks on its sides. Unfortunately, this wonderfully restored interior sits homeless, in packing cases in a suburban Glasgow warehouse.

The most remarkable of the Cranston tea rooms was the last in the series and the only one which partly remains and is partly in use today: The Willow. Here CRM remodelled the facade and amended the structure as well as carving out and linking the interiors. With the theme from Sauchiehall, which is said to mean 'street of the willow', the interior design was built around lines of Dante Gabriel Rossetti:

'Oh ye, all ye that walk in Willowwood
that walk with hollow faces burning bright...'

The willow tree and its leaf are behind all the imagery, often abstracted to an extreme, as seen in two ground floor elements: first, the lattice back of the curved settle which, separating front and back diners, was the order-desk chair (now in the Art School), and second, the extraordinary plaster panelled frieze round the wall (discussed on p68).

The ground floor front and back saloons, and the top-lit mezzanine gallery at the back, made three interrelated but distinct places. The street front, in silver, white and rose, was the Ladies' Tea Room; the dark Luncheon Room for men and women was behind; the Tea Gallery above, a rose-bower in pink, white and grey. Then, on the first floor, overlooking Sauchiehall Street, was the

Ladies' Room, a silvery willow grove, the exquisite 'Salon de Luxe'. This Room de Luxe was entered through glazed double doors, the most simple and straightforward in form, but now among the most famously decorated doors in the world. Further up, behind windows whose section above the encircling doorhead rail was deeply recessed (forming lovely, low window bays), were found the dark stained and panelled Billiard and Smoking

Rooms, with motifs of applied squares. In the basement (and actually next door), shortly before the First World War ground to an end, CRM added another room, 'The Dug Out'.

Two rooms, the back gallery and Room de Luxe, were reopened in 1983, after extensive restoration by Geoffrey Wimpenny (of Keppie Henderson, descendant of Honeyman, Keppie & Mackintosh). So today we enter through Henderson's, a jewellery and gift shop of trinkets and uncontrolled reflections. The top-lit back gallery, held on great steel joists, has the eight tapering columns (note their capitals); there once were, also, vertical rows of more tiny squares; symbolic trees simply supporting the ceiling grid of enclosing foliage.

The Willow Tea Rooms façade detail, showing the 'fenêtre en longeur' (the room-wide window) of the Room de Luxe from outside.

Further up we reach the Room de Luxe, until recently entered through magnificent glazed doors. The shapes and colours of their leaded lights can entrance the eye for hours; to see them swing as waitresses bring through the tea-trays, and how different they look from different sides and in different lights! (These doors were removed to travel with the 1996 exhibition, and were to be

back in place, in their original and everyday – their extraordinary and exotic and magical – use by now. But their fragility has made that hope unrealistic; they may be exhibited somewhere within the Willow building rather than be reinstated.) They remain CRM's most elaborate essay in stained and leaded glass.

Here the chairs today, in their aluminium paint, seem stage props, clumsy reproductions; yet in fact the originals, silver-painted and upholstered in purple velvet, were very similar. (Originally only eight of these tall chairs stood at formally aligned central tables, surrounded by others with lower backs. Today's scatter and randomly placed tables offers a quite different spatial sense.) The colour scheme of silver and purple, while feminine, has moved on from CRM's white rooms designed in the year or two before: and the space is architecturally, rather than decoratively composed.

The elegance is held by the precise spatial control: the low cornice at doorhead onto which rests the barrel ceiling is a rail which runs all round, holding together the lower walls of mirrored and leaded panes separated by thin white vertical bands, below which the walls were upholstered in pale grey silk, stitched with beads; the banquette seat backs in purple velvet. The vault comes down to the low street windows, each casement with its hearts of silver mirror. The endlessly reflective complexity dissolves the edges of this stylised grove into the distance. Only the high flat cap of the fireplace and, opposite it, of the frame for MMM's gesso panel based on the Rossetti sonnet just touch the ceiling's barrel, breaking the implied lowness of the space, down to which the groups of four-square light fittings drop. (MMM's gesso, *Oh, ye that walk in Willowwood*, like the doors, was exhibited with the 1996 Glasgow exhibition and has not yet returned home. It also may end up as part of a display elsewhere within the building.)

Originally a central chandelier was made up of myriad rose-coloured glass baubles on strings surrounding a large bulb. It has long since vanished. That's a pity, for seeing it, and other details from this interior, like the strings of glass balls in the balcony edging which are preserved at the Hunterian, would make us wonder how close we are sailing here to the tawdry.

On opening in October 1903, the Willow interior was an immediate cause célèbre. It is strange to imagine this fairy place of pearls and roses as purveyor of teas, scrambled eggs and mutton pies to everyday Glaswegian folk. An amusing contemporary tale by my aunt's father, Neil Munro (written for the *Glasgow Evening News* at the time) charmingly encapsulates an ordinary pair's first experience of this 'Room de Looks'. In the end, 'when the pie cam' up, it was jist the shape o' an ordinary pie, wi' nae beads nor anything Airt about it, and Duffy cheered up at that, and said he enjoyed his tea.'

◀ *Looking through the wonderful glazed doors into the Room de Luxe (1903). Today the light fittings visible beyond are very similar to those CRM used widely elsewhere, from his own house to the Ingram Street Ladies' Luncheon Room. Of the original fitment which hung centrally in the Room de Luxe, with its drops of pink glass, Neil Munro's Duffy asked: 'What are all these drips and dangles?', to which his companion replied: 'Airt, that's Airt.'*

SCHOOLS

CRM designed two schools; the first, Martyrs' Public School (1895), when he was Honeyman and Keppie's assistant in charge. It closely resembles the plan and organisation type of the conventional small board schools of its time. If you could get inside (and it is now in public ownership, though probably to remain in use by the Museums

conservation department), Martyrs' would show the typical educational environment of a century ago. Symmetrical, with boys' and girls' entrances to east and west giving to the central hall, off which – and off its upper floor galleries – are three layers of conventional classrooms. CRM's signature is suggested by the art nouveau motifs around the entrances, and on the timber eaves which fly out over the stairhead windows. The overall form is rather clumsy and boxy. Internal details, restored and refurbished, add touches of charm: the metal balustrade brackets, the wall tiles, the glazed wooden screens.

It is really only in the roof trusses, and especially

Above: the early Martyrs' School. Opposite: one of the soaring stair towers of Scotland Street School (1906), showing the extraordinary, daring precision of masonry and glass, under its conical slate hat.

the six closely spaced trusses over the stair, which seem pegged in a Japanese manner, that the designer's character shows through. Here we learn a little more about Mackintosh: for during renovation work which removed plaster from the stair head, it became clear that the pairs of brackets which seem to hold the truss ends, as if pegged to the ends of double beams, are merely short decorative additions. The visible structure is interesting timberwork; but some other interesting timberwork is simply meant to look like structure!

Mackintosh began to design the Scotland Street School in 1903; it was completed, 25% over budget, in 1906. The planning, as with all CRM plans, is absolutely within the given tradition. Two great stair towers on the front (one over the boys' one the girls' entrance), flank the hall above which sit two layers of classrooms. The vast vaulted cookery room at the top, where a 23 ft (7 m) long dresser and a cabinet by CRM remain, fills the length between the stair towers; it is worth the climb. Seen from the front, thinner, stepped layers of cloakrooms are next to the stair towers, with staff rooms at the outer ends. On the back, absolutely directly, we see three layers of six classrooms, each with three windows. Only minimal decoration (including some green-glazed surfaces) articulates the centre and end bays with abstract, geometrical tree and thistle.

This ambiguity of front and back – the classically symmetrical southern side, the stair towers and other additive bits to the north – is played quite faintly. Moreover, while the curving glazed towers suggest the winding stair of the traditonal Scottish country house, here the plan is quite different. Straight flights and landings stand back from the bay, leaving great semi-circular wells of light between outside and in. Inside these towers, note the spare, elegant joinery above, the metal ties, circles and rods; and once you're up there, enjoy the magnificent view north across Glasgow.

▶ *The centre of the south façade of Scotland Street School, seen from the playground at the back, but designed ambiguously like a front. This articulation of form, the plasticity of red stone and shadow with spots of green glaze (centring on an abstract thistle symbolising Scotland), is one of CRM's most unprecedented and satisfying surface treatments.*

The central hall is surrounded by white tiled 'windows' and blue tiled columns, all with green trim. Rather than being conventionally enclosed by walls, this space is articulated by sinking the hall four steps below the main noisy thoroughfare of children, and beyond a row of piers; by having side bays on the ground floor between deep fins (like theatrical boxes); and by the columns set back from the mezzanine balcony edge. All this creates a wonderfully useful theatrical space.

For the rest, the magic is in the detail. At the entrances, note how CRM, mannerist as ever, has classical details drape over the porches like tasselled tablecloths. Then look up at the pinched peaks of the masonry columns under the attic storey. The decorative treatment at the significant places of the building – entrances, stairs and where it hits the sky – shows CRM now at his most abstract. As you leave, note the formal composition of the caretaker's house; look at the wall and fence, in such elegant daring masonry and metal; and see the pattern of almost square shapes on the railings: an abstraction of thistle seeds, symbolising the children as Scotland's future.

THE MACKINTOSH HOUSE

There are no original houses by CRM left in Glasgow. Hous'hill, Miss Cranston's home, was destroyed, the Mackintoshes' own house demolished. But the latter is rebuilt, using genuine interiors, within the University of Glasgow (Hunterian Art Gallery) Mackintosh Collection; while a House for an Art Lover has recently been constructed in Bellahouston Park.

So, as chimerical as the tea rooms, the domestic interiors of Mackintosh have had a remarkable ability to dissolve and reappear in front of our eyes. Even the room which 'The Four' created for the Vienna exhibition in 1900 was reconstructed in Edinburgh in the 1980s, but as soon vanished again.

The Mackintosh House in the Hunterian Art Gallery brings us, through various veils, to how they lived ('they', for it is as surely the result of MMM's sensibility as CRM's alone). Rebuilt only a few metres from its original site, most of the interior we see here – the actual fitments, from freestanding bed or sideboard to the fitted fireplaces – had already been moved by the Mackintoshes themselves, from the Blythswood Square flat which they had fitted out on their marriage in 1900.

Contemporary photographs of that earlier flat show the fine classical Glaswegian drawing room, transformed. The space was emptied of late Victorian clutter, and lowered by an enclosing rail. This ran along walls and, where it crossed the windows already diffused with taut white muslin, it dropped translucent veils embroidered (we guess) in pale purple and/or green. Narrow gas pipes are taken in decorative loops across the ceiling from the central rose to wonderful drop fittings in the corners, softly to illuminate the whiteness. The walls are panels of grey canvas against each of which stood one important designed element: fireplace, desk

◀ The drawing room (recreated as 1906). Interior architecture is the great synthetic art. Its popularity a century ago created cluttered, fin-de-siècle jungles. But CRM cut through the confusion. Here the enclosing rail lowers the Victorian window-head (to the left) and ties in the new window (to the right) which he cut in the gable wall 'for my wife Margaret, so that she can watch the sunsets.'. Onto the refined spatial order, CRM layered surface detail of coloured glass, fabric, embroidery or stencil; and then the moveable pieces which altogether complete the design.

or bookcase. The dining room is smaller and almost like a shrine, with its wall candles, dark wood furniture and walls lined with coarse, dark wrapping-paper. The white bedroom, though spatially insignificant, is filled with organic forms decorating the white furniture offset by coloured glass; here was the elegant foundation of CRM's European fame in those next few years.

All this came with them when they moved in 1906 to Gilmorehill and thence to be rebuilt in 1981. Today, entering the typical, narrow and tall hall of this mid-nineteenth century terrace – from the Hunterian, as we must – you see the inside of the front door, with its four square lenses, the panelling bellying out towards the reformed window and mirror opposite, held together by the dark framing at door height – all touches aimed at widening and lowering the sense of this tunnel. Simple austerity is offset by the petal wall lamps (which had been exhibited in The Rose Boudoir in Turin in 1902). Before passing, look again at the large mirror, designed for their own use by MMM (with her sister and brother-in-law). This strange design in beaten lead, the first and last view of themselves at the point of transition to the public world, represents what? With its peacock tails above and below, but even more the fish leaping in front of bearded profiles mirrored left and right.

Next door, the small dark dining room is muted; dull walls clothed in a black trellis with stylised pink roses are offset wonderfully with silver drops of rain, or cherry blossom in a wind. Windows and door seem left untouched. The dark chairs (first designed as architectural bodies shaping places in the Argyle Street tea rooms) complement the table and sideboard which the Mackintoshes designed for themselves.

Upstairs, we open the only door, small in scale and inset with 20 of the loveliest pink glass tears (though we really only see their quality from the other side), to enter the L-shaped room, looking

▶ *The dark-painted and virtually unaltered dining room. The focus is on the dining table, which would have been laid with CRM-designed silver-ware and lit from CRM-designed candle-sticks. The room builds a subtle palette of browns with (out of the picture) the dark trellis and CRM fireplace, set off by spots of silver.*

through from the cool studio to the sunnier glow of the drawing room. As theirs was the end-of-terrace house, CRM could create a long first-floor window in the south-facing gable wall; this, and the removal of other doors and partitions on this floor, transformed it into a quite unexpected place.

The mood here is an utter contrast to that below: a white, spacious calm fills the space. The wall between the two rooms is pulled up to stop at the band which runs round the entire area at door-head. This band, so close above the head (and appearing very differently from the many low-angle photographs often published) frames and encloses the space remarkably, while also extending it hor-

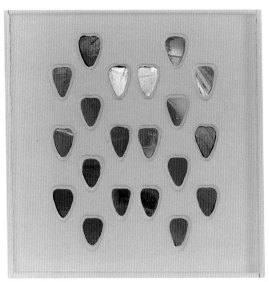

Detail of the door to the first floor room, whose colours change as you move past and the door moves open.

izontally. Where it runs across the tall study window, this band offers translucent pink and purple squares; where it runs across the drawing-room's typical Victorian bay window, a wall drops down to it, tightening the horizontal geometry of the room (and creating of the window bay an extraordinary place to be in!). The high window representing 'studio' is not just a conversion necessity: exactly the same device is used to represent 'library' at the new-built Hill House, where the window rises above the enclosing rail. Of the other windows, the rail forms the heads; particularly the new long set of small-pane, leaded casements, which, quite differently from the large pane Victorian sashes at the front, attract the body to approach, open, and look out at Gilbert Scott's romantic university turrets.

The division of spaces down to a rail at door-head is a powerful Japanese domestic tradition. While CRM may have seen memories of this in Smith & Brewer's Mary Ward House in London (1895), no contemporary designer articulated it as he did. The potentially linked Art School studios show one extreme; this subtle restructuring of the first floor of his own home is brilliantly convincing. Light floods into this space, diffused through muslin, to show up the many remarkable objects and elements within. These are all well described for visitors, but any can repay close attention. I will mention a very few.

In the studio is the yin and yang pair, the bookcase and writing desk. On the white, low cur-vaceous bookcase (of 1900), its sinuous plants and tear drops in front of the four full moons is a par-ticularly subtle essay in leaded stained glass. As with the 1902 drawing room cabinet next door, the material just happens to be wood; the luxuri-ous, curvilinear surfaces mask inevitably difficult wooden junctions under thickly lacquered paint. The black writing cabinet, standing with its doors open (like an open kimono) is its dark, geometric twin. Designed for Hill House in 1904, the original is perhaps the masterpiece among CRM's furni-ture. This is the copy which CRM-MMM had made for themselves. Here luxury is in the material, which is not hidden. Woods are carefully chosen and revealed, the mother-of-pearl squares of squares, the formal geometry, is always softened with tiny touches, with ivory and with the central metal panel decorated eloquently (and differently from The Hill House original) with the crying rose in leaded glass. These two pieces are wonderfully complementary, but they also show just how CRM's designing had moved within those few years from the 1900 style which brought him

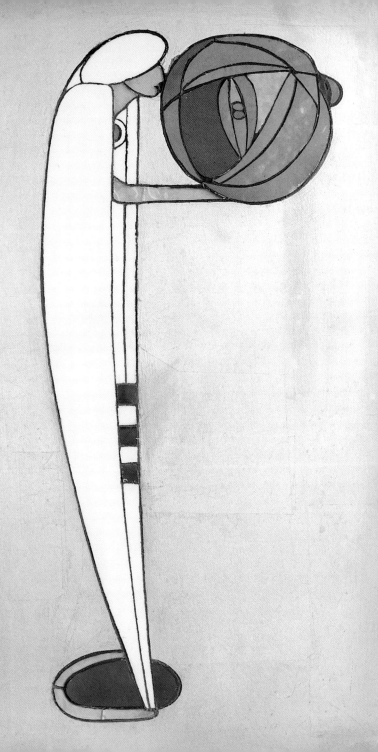

instant fame to the controlled maturity of 1904.

Above the fireplace stands MMM's gesso (plaster) panel called *The White Rose and The Red Rose*. Look closely, for no photograph does justice to this delicate richness; the face, the beads, the scrim, as it catches this pale light.

Through to the drawing room, look at the white desk, and the doors on its front, with women and roses, as ever, on MMM's silvered copper panels. Note the exquisite tiny circular table in the corner; thickly lacquered, brilliantly shaped, and easily overlooked. These are indeed sensuous surfaces. As Alan Crawford rightly notes, 'visitors wait until the attendant looks away, and then touch them,

stroking the silky surfaces as they would stroke a lover, exploring, looking for reassurance.' Today CRM's objects, designed to enrich their users' everyday experiences, are transformed into museum valuables and we must resist the temptation to make contact with them! But look even more closely at the forms; how sections change as they rise from the floor (the dining room chairs were also a good example), or how the support of the weight of table-top or cabinet is expressed.

There is no warm clutter; no patterned wallpaper, upholstery or rugs. We might contrast this turn-of-the-century interior with the National Trust

Opposite: drawing room cabinet doors (1902); the stylised woman and rose may have been formed by MMM in coloured glass on the silvered doors. Above: MMM gesso panel above studio mantelpiece.

for Scotland's 'tenement flat', on Garnet Hill, only two minutes' walk from the Art School (a typical, small petit-bourgeois flat of the same moment). In the Mackintosh house all is Art. Yet it is not extravagant – it is very often the cheap luxury of cream paint and coloured glass and enamel. But it is also of purity of space, simplicity of form, economy of

means, as in the aesthetic dried flower arrangements.

Going up one more flight, we recognise the stairhead plaster panel placed here by CRM; it is from the frieze back in place on the ground floor of the Willow Tea Rooms. Of these panels (from 1903-4), Nikolaus Pevsner said, 'he discovered the necessity and possibility of abstract art in his wall panels several years before Picasso and Kandinsky had begun their efforts to liberate art from nature.' Perhaps this panel is

The tiny clock (1905) on the mantelpiece in the drawing room; a version of one designed by CRM for The Hill House.

indeed where we can best apply art historical terms like 'pioneer' to Mackintosh. The category of being 'first' doesn't seem very useful in approaching an artist's work, least of all CRM, whose goals were quite different. But here the date is important. Perhaps I find the panel incongruous here because the rest of this house was built of ideas (and indeed of many physical bits) which are a few years older; CRM of the Willow and The Hill House had been moving on from the home he was here recreating with MMM. The tale of this panel as liberating abstraction is, however, more ambiguous. For CRM's drawing of the frieze shows it coloured, decorated and filled towards the top with densely packed pink roses. (Ah, says Billcliffe; but in making it, CRM resisted what was 'almost certainly Margaret's influence and tendency to apply pattern and decoration to every square inch.') A fine work of art, as always, offers a silent mirror to the viewer, in which to see his (in these

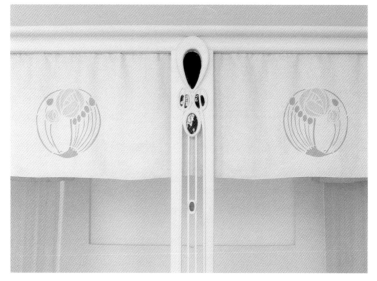

cases) own views of Modernism, sexism or whatever.

On the second floor, the partition is again removed and a smaller L-shaped room results, formed by its architectonic objects – the fireplace, the cheval mirror (the very one which was in the room setting in Vienna in 1900) and the great bed designed for their marriage in 1900, (all of which came from the Mains Street flat, all capped at the same height, of an upstretched arm).

Note the tiny glass lenses on the central bed-end, which, in the morning sun, cast coloured light onto the bed. Look here at the beautiful birds (are they doves?) on the wardrobe, their claws

Detail of the first four-poster bed CRM designed, for his marriage to Margaret Macdonald in 1900.

stretching down to form the handles. See the carved plant motif on the tables, as they run down to the floor at the corners of the legs; and again look at the gorgeous lights: orange glowing within brazen cubes of metal with a tear drop in each side and their enclosing saucer above.

Having failed to get to the attic bedroom up the smaller stair with its surprising black and white vertical striped wallpaper, we try the bathroom door and are astonished to find ourselves in the gallery, a bizarre and tall new space. We have moved from a Mackintosh space to the world of exhibited artifacts. The Hunterian holds over 600 Mackintosh drawings and designs, as well as 30 important pieces of furniture, and else besides including work of MMM and their twin couple in The Four, her sister Frances and husband Herbert McNair (whose son donated many of the items, from the Mackintosh estate).

So here is exhibited a changing collection of furniture, drawings, banners and paintings. There are touches of the decorative layers of the Willow Tea Rooms – chequered and willowleaf pattern leaded glass panels (set high up in the walls to the left); and fragments from the balcony edge – sparse, flat steels with square punched holes and thin bent rods with green glass drops and vertical strings of glass balls.

Often on display, and worth looking for, is an absolutely stunning table, in mahogany and with a pearl dot drawer handle, designed in 1912 for his friend William Douglas, who as a decorator had worked on various CRM projects. Its eight, elegant, aerofoil legs stand four in corners and four between the spreading spokes halfway to the centre. At the centre, these spokes rise into a tower lattice with its very 'constructional' (half-notched) joints. This is as subtle, complex and satisfying as the 1908 cube table at The Hill House, and much less well-known.

In addition to this scatter of exhibits, here is also

► *Derngate guest bedroom (1919). The geometric decoration almost turns the room into one four-poster bed. With their severe forms, enlivened just by the grain, black edging and ultramarine stencilled chequers and the squares of mother-of-pearl on the handles, these oak pieces were made by German prisoners-of-war on the Isle of Man in 1917.*

the complete guest bedroom from 78 Derngate: dazzling black, white and ultramarine stripes (in a tiny room), which frame the simple oak furniture. The bedside chest, with six little drawers, five long ones and a top-opening cabinet, is a perfect engineer's tool box! When on one occasion Bassett-Lowke's guest George Bernard Shaw was asked if the jarring decoration in this room hadn't disturbed his sleep, Shaw replied that it was no problem. He always slept with his eyes shut.

Having descended again, the abiding image of this visit to the Mackintosh house is of the drawing room and studio; that white space. Did Margaret really paint her etiolated gesso maidens while wearing kid gloves, standing on a white carpet? In this world which 'cannot tolerate an intrusion of the ordinary' (to quote Hermann Muthesius, their key contemporary German supporter and friend), where is the space for everyday life?

Yet that question might seem strange to a Japanese, from whose culture CRM took such inspiration. In Japan, not only are restraint, subtlety of form and surface, and economy of means prized, but the flower arrangement or the bowl on the table are as much art work as the paintings on the wall. In our era of 'minimalism' as high taste this is far from news; but in Glasgow a century ago it was revolutionary.

INFORMATION DIRECTORY

To visit on foot:

Glasgow School of Art, 167 Renfrew Street, Glasgow G3 6RQ. Still a working Art School; access by guided tour only, usually twice each day, once on Saturday and none on Sunday. The best time to get a fuller view of this building in use is at the annual exhibition of student work in June. (Beware that it may be totally closed the previous week for external examinations.) All dates and times are worth checking in advance. Telephone: 0141 353 4526; Fax 0141 353 4746.

Queen's Cross Church, now headquarters of the Charles Rennie Mackintosh Society, 870 Garscube Road, Glasgow G20 7EL; open Mon to Fri 10-5, Sat 10-2 and Sun 2-5. With the co-operation of all those involved with the Mackintosh heritage, the CRM Society is able to arrange guided tours – write, fax or telephone for details. Tel 0141 946 6600; Fax 0141 945 2321; email info@crmsociety.com

Ruchill Church Hall, Shakespeare Street, Glasgow G20 9PT. This busy hall, not far from Queen's Cross Church, is open for viewing Mon to Fri 10.30-2.30; enquire at the Church House in the courtyard.

Windyhill, Kilmacolm, is not open to the public and can only be seen from the public road.

The House for an Art Lover, Bellahouston Park, Dumbreck Road, Glasgow G41 5BW; exhibition, café and design shop open daily 10.00 to 5.00, admission £3.50 concessions £2.50. Telephone: information 0141 353 4449; or 0141 353 4770; Fax 0141 353 4771.

The Hill House, Helensburgh, Strathclyde, G84 9AJ, approximately 23 miles NW of Glasgow; just over a mile uphill from Helensburgh station (up Sinclair Street, over the railway by the Upper Station, then left into Upper Colquhoun Street). Owned by The National Trust for Scotland. Open daily April to October in the afternoons, although access is restricted at peak times, and visitors may have to wait until others have left. Telephone 01436 673900.

Willow Tea Rooms, 217 Sauchiehall Street, Glasgow G2 3EX. Open for light meals and tea normal shopping hours; telephone 0141 332 0521.

Ingram Street Tea Rooms. The Chinese Room, having been partially reconstructed, is now undergoing complete restoration, following the example of the beautifully restored Ladies' Luncheon Room, which has been on tour with the CRM 1996 Exhibition. For current information telephone Glasgow Museums, 0141 287 2699.

Miss Cranston had opened a tea room at 205 Ingram Street in 1885 and by 1907 had aquired the whole block, 205-217. CRM designed a number of interconnecting rooms, beginning with The Ladies' Luncheon Room in 1900. In 1907 he added an Oak Room, fronting onto Miller Street. Like the Ladies' Luncheon Room, this too had a double columned space at the street; but unlike it, this one carried a gallery, inevitably blocking light from getting deeper into space. In 1909, he designed the Oval Room and Ladies' Rest Room; in 1911 he designed the Chinese Room. Here there was a dark ceiling hidden by a bright blue horizontal lattice, square trellis work and deep strong colours. Up till 1911, CRM had used colour very sparingly. Suddenly we have bright blues and reds on black; it is dark and exotic. The next, and last room at Ingram Street, the altered Cloister Room of 1912 is quite different again. This low barrel vault (which hid an earlier CRM decorative scheme) had layered wall panels of shiny, waxed wood, decorated with delicate vertical strips of harlequin lozenges painted red, green and blue, and with much mirror glass round its low vault. There are what look like round-headed double doors (or recessed panels?) covered in thin strips of leaded mirror under an extraordinary, melting doorhead. Was this a totally new, restless space developing from the recently completed Art School library? When we see this mysterious room restored, our views of Mackintosh will surely change. Here was a quite different exoticism, a taste of cosmopolitan Vienna.

The Argyle Street Tea Rooms may have left us only furniture; but the amazing range of interior spaces from Ingram Street survived. They were closed in 1949 and bought grudgingly by the city in 1950 (under pressure from Thomas Howarth and others). The building had become an unloved, tawdry, tartan souvenir store when I was a student, cruelly called The Charles Rennie Mackintosh Discount Warehouse. The interiors were finally removed and stored in 1971. Glasgow Museums wouldn't take responsibility, and neglect led to scandalous decay. Finally Glasgow began making magnificent amends, and we eagerly await the complete repair and public display of these interiors. The Ladies' Luncheon Room raises high hopes; CRM's Ingram Street interiors have been awarded Heritage Lottery funds to be restored. Options for the future display of the tea rooms are being explored by Glasgow Museums and other agencies in the city.

Kelvingrove Art Gallery & Museum has a Glasgow Style gallery which exhibits Ingram Street Tea Room furniture, amidst other work by CRM and his contemporaries in Glasgow. For current information telephone Glasgow Museums, 0141 287 2699.

Scotland Street School, 225 Scotland Street, Glasgow G5 8QB. Closed as a school in 1979. Since 1990, The Museum of Education, open Monday to Thursday, and Saturday 10.00 to 5.00, and Friday and Sunday 1.00 to 5.00; admission free. Telephone: 0141 287 0500; Fax: 0141 287 0515.

Martyrs' Public School, Parson Street / 11 Barony Street, Glasgow G4 OPX. Saved in 1970s by public protest from demolition in the line of an inner ring motorway now stopped. Restored for Glasgow Museums, open daily 1.00 to 4.00. For information telephone 0141 287 8621.

The Mackintosh House, Hunterian Art Gallery, University of Glasgow, Hillhead Street, Glasgow G12 8QQ. The Mackintosh Gallery has changing exhibitions. The reserve collection holds up to 800 sheets of CRM drawings, including flower drawings and related material, to which access is available by appointment. Open Mon to Sat but closed for lunch. Confirm opening times in advance; telephone: 0141 330 5431; Fax 0141 330 3618; Web-site http://www.gla.ac.uk/Museum/

Places not discussed include:

140-2 Balgrayhill Road (1890). CRM's first known work; very ordinary semi-detached houses designed for relatives.

Craigie Hall, 6 Rowan Road, Glasgow G41 5BS. Designed by Honeyman (1872) and extended by Keppie and his assistant CRM. Detailing on the doorcases and in the library (1892-3) is probably CRM's; the music room and organ case (1897) certainly are. A professional office not normally open to the public.

Queen Margaret Ladies' College (1894-5). Queen Margaret Drive. Designed by Keppie with CRM; now surrounded by BBC buildings and only visible from their stairwell.

Glasgow Herald **Building** (1893-4), Mitchell Street. CRM's first big architectural job; a simple newspaper distribution warehouse whose only particular requirements were a water tower (important fire precaution) and a clear route through the middle of the ground floor for dispatch vans. For the idea of the corner tower, CRM returned to his storehouse of travel sketches and, on blank sheets in his Italian sketchbook of 1891, he made the first sketch designs for

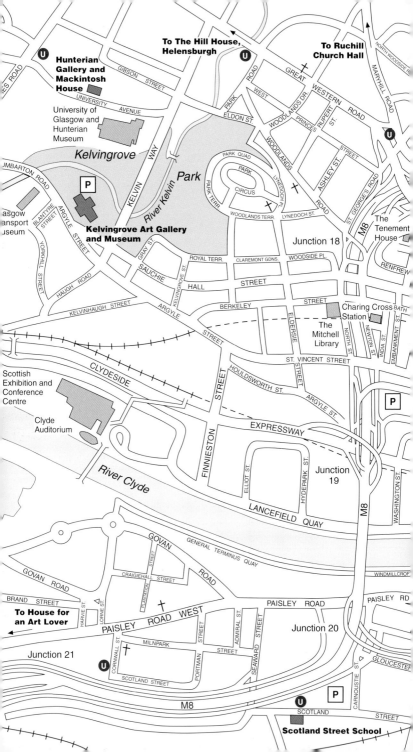

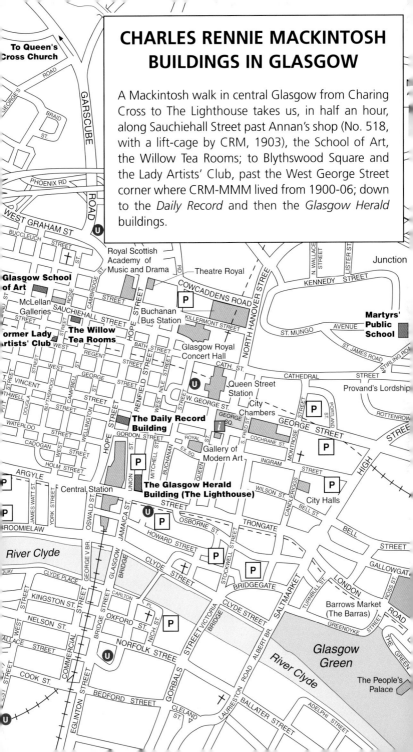

CHARLES RENNIE MACKINTOSH BUILDINGS IN GLASGOW

A Mackintosh walk in central Glasgow from Charing Cross to The Lighthouse takes us, in half an hour, along Sauchiehall Street past Annan's shop (No. 518, with a lift-cage by CRM, 1903), the School of Art, the Willow Tea Rooms; to Blythswood Square and the Lady Artists' Club, past the West George Street corner where CRM-MMM lived from 1900-06; down to the *Daily Record* and then the *Glasgow Herald* buildings.

To Queen's Cross Church

GARSCUBE ROAD

GEORGE'S

BRAID ST.

PHOENIX RD.

WEST GRAHAM ST.

BUCCLEUCH STREET

Royal Scottish Academy of Music and Drama

Theatre Royal

COWCADDENS ROAD

KENNEDY STREET

N. WALLACE STREET

LISTER STREET

Junction

Glasgow School of Art

McLellan Galleries

SAUCHIEHALL STREET

CAMBRIDGE STREET

ROSE STREET

HOPE STREET

Buchanan Bus Station

KILLERMONT STREET

NORTH HANOVER STREET

ST. MUNGO AVENUE

Martyrs' Public School

Former Lady Artists' Club

The Willow Tea Rooms

WEST REGENT STREET

BATH STREET

Glasgow Royal Concert Hall

CATH. ST.

ST. JAMES ROAD

CATHEDRAL STREET

STIRLING RD.

WEST GEORGE STREET

VINCENT

BLYTHSWOOD

CAMPBELL ST.

RENFIELD STREET

WEST NILE STREET

HOPE STREET

W. GEORGE ST.

Queen Street Station

City Chambers

PORTLAND ST.

Provand's Lordship

ROTTENROW

THWELL

DOUGLAS

WATERLOO STREET

WELLINGTON STREET

The Daily Record Building

GORDON STREET

ROYAL EX. SQ.

GEORGE SQ.

i

GEORGE STREET

COCHRANE STREET

MONTROSE STREET

P

STREET

HIGH STREET

CADOGAN STREET

HOLM STREET

MITCHELL ST.

BUCHANAN

QUEEN STREET

Gallery of Modern Art

INGRAM STREET

P

ARGYLE STREET

JAMES WATT ST.

YORK STREET

Central Station

OSWALD ST.

UNION ST.

The Glasgow Herald Building (The Lighthouse)

WILSON ST.

CANDLERIGGS

BELL ST.

City Halls

P

ROOMIELAW

JAMAICA ST.

STREET

OSBORNE ST.

HOWARD STREET

TRONGATE

BELL STREET

GALLOWGAT

River Clyde

CLYDE PLACE

KINGSTON ST.

NELSON ST.

GEORGE V BR.

GLASGOW BRIDGE

BRIDGE STREET

CARLTON PL.

CLYDE STREET

STOCKWELL STREET

BRIDGEGATE

SALTMARKET

TURNBULL ST.

LONDON ROAD

Barrows Market (The Barras)

GREENDYKE STREET

THE GREEN

ROSS ST.

WALLACE STREET

COOK ST.

COMMERCIAL STREET

OXFORD ST.

NICH. ST.

NORFOLK STREE

GORBALS

BEDFORD STREET

VICTORIA BRIDGE

CLYDE STREET

ALBERT BR.

River Clyde

Glasgow Green

The People's Palace

EGLINTON STREET

CLELAND ST.

LAURIESTON ROAD

BALLATER STREET

ADELPHI STREET

the *Herald* tower. On the most prominent corner, the tower is dramatically visible; the stonework on the facade is well worth a close look. Now known as The Lighthouse, it was recreated by architects Page & Park as Glasgow's centre for architecture and design in 1999. Included is The Mackintosh Interpretation Centre, a permanent exhibition of CRM's work and influence. From this exhibition there is access to the corner tower with wonderful views across and beyond the city. For information telephone 0141 221 6362.

Daily Record **Building** (1900-1) Renfield Lane. A conventional warehouse and print works, CRM's effort being concentrated on the surface to this narrow lane. It is clad in white glazed bricks. If this is presumably to increase reflected illumination, that will help only the opposite neighbours. For CRM it is a play on image, as ever; here the image is that of the enclosed light-well of Edwardian blocks (which never appear on an outside!). The ground floor, however, is a grey sandstone arcade; the undulating heads very minimally formed and exquisitely precise, the shapes of capital, keystone, arch, implied most economically – apart from the doorway whose mannerism is a brilliant play of forms, thrown away down this narrow lane.

Looking upwards, the bays of the surface are articulated simply; the dotted green bricks topped with red triangles, as stylized trees, carry the eye up to the sky, where we glimpse a great cap of stone waves and a baronial turret!

An Artist's Country Cottage, uncommissioned project published by CRM in Germany (1902); recreated from these drawings 90 years later at Strathnairn, 7 miles south of Inverness.

The Lady Artists' Club (1908), 5 Blythswood Square. See how CRM stuck a wonderful black classic portico in a round-headed entrance. Where he also worked in the hallway and ground floor this is now a private office.

78 Derngate, Northampton (1916 and later). Guided by a Trust, supported by a Friends committee, and with designs by architect John McAslan, ambitious plans to restore this fascinating but tiny property are underway. Public access will be possible on occasions as work progresses. For information contact the Trust at 01604 494056 (telephone and fax), e-mail: i.t.p@btinternet.com, web: www.78derngate.org.uk

Gourock Parish Church, down the Clyde, south-west of Glasgow, has an indifferent pulpit and choir stalls by CRM (1899).

Holy Trinity Church, 12 Keir Street, Bridge of Allan, Stirling. Pulpit, communion table and organ screen (1904), richly carved in oak in CRM's unique, organic Gothic exuberance. Usually open on Saturdays 10am-4pm, between 1 June and 30 September; telephone 01786 832093 or 834155.

To visit in armchair: Fine story, up-to-date scholarship and good value for money: *Charles Rennie Mackintosh*, Alan Crawford, London, 1995 (paperback); *Charles Rennie Mackintosh*, essays edited by Wendy Kaplan, Abbeville Press / Glasgow Museums, New York and Glasgow, 1996. Best for your coffee table: *Remembering Charles Rennie Mackintosh*, Alistair Moffat, Colin Baxter, Lanark, 1989; *Charles Rennie Mackintosh: Synthesis in Form*, James Steele (words) and Eric Thorburn (photographs), London, 1994. For ideas: *Charles Rennie Mackintosh: The Poetics of Workmanship*, David Brett, London, 1992 and *Part Seen, Part Imagined*, Timothy Neat, Edinburgh, 1994. For a story of his life: *Charles Rennie Mackintosh, Architect, Artist, Icon*, John McKean and Colin Baxter, Edinburgh, 2000.

Glasgow School of Art: Five studies, quite different and not all equally accessible: William Buchanan (Ed.), *Mackintosh's Masterwork*, Glasgow, 1989; Robert Harbison, 'The Glasgow School of Art: Master of Building', in *The Architects' Journal*, 14 June 1989, and Mark Girouard, 'The Glasgow School of Art', in Kaplan (editor) 1996; James Macaulay, *Glasgow School of Art*, London, 1993. *GA49: Glasgow School of Art*, Japan, 1979, with a brief essay by Andy MacMillan.

The House for an Art Lover: *Charles Rennie Mackintosh*, Meister der Innen Kunst 2 – Haus Eines Kunstfreundes, Verlag Alex, Koch Darmstadt. The published document on which the new House for an Art Lover was recreated. A modern facsimile of this original portfolio of drawings with text in English by H. Muthesius is in print, but not cheap. On the other hand, the complete set is well reproduced in Steele (see above).

The Hill House: John McKean, 'The Hill House' in Kaplan (editor) 1996; James Macaulay, *The Hill House*, London, 1994; *The Hill House*, NTS booklet with text by Roger Billcliffe (and Anne Ellis).

Tea Rooms: Alan Crawford, 'The Tea Rooms: Art and Domesticity', in Kaplan (editor), 1996; Perilla Kinchin,*Taking Tea with Mackintosh,* San Francisco, 1998. For a wider context see this author's *Tea and Taste, Glasgow Tea Rooms 1875–1975*, Oxon, 1991.

Scotland Street School: Gavin Stamp, 'Scotland Street School: Master of Building', in *The Architects' Journal*, 6.4.1988.

The Mackintosh House: Pamela Robertson, *The Mackintosh House*, Glasgow, 1998, is an exquisitely beautiful souvenir of the building.

Painting, Furniture and Collaboration

This guide to CRM's spatial and built designs has only mentioned moveable works where they are accessible in Glasgow; therefore it has not focused on drawings, paintings or furniture in themselves. They are well covered in key references.

Painting: Roger Billcliffe, *Charles Rennie Mackintosh, Architectural Sketches and Flower Drawings*, London, 1977 and his *Mackintosh Watercolours*, (3rd ed) London, 1993; Pamela Robertson, *Charles Rennie Mackintosh: Art is the Flower*, London, 1995.

Furniture: Roger Billcliffe, *Charles Rennie Mackintosh, the Complete Furniture, Furniture Drawings and Interior Designs*, (3rd ed), London, 1986.

Textiles: Roger Billcliffe, *Mackintosh Textile Designs*, San Francisco, 1993.

Margaret Macdonald: Her particular contribution is well contextualised in Jude Burkhauser (editor), *The Glasgow Girls*, Edinburgh, 1990.

Index